I AM GOD Almighty

Is Anything Too Hard for Me?

Chantal Kaberuka

I AM GOD ALMIGHTY
Copyright © 2023 by Chantal Kaberuka

Scripture quotations marked (NKJV) taken from the New King James Version®. Copyright © 1982 by Thomas Nelson. Used by permission. All rights reserved. Scripture quotations marked (NIV) are taken from the Holy Bible, New International Version®, NIV®. Copyright © 1973, 1978, 1984, 2011 by Biblica, Inc.™ Used by permission of Zondervan. All rights reserved worldwide. www.zondervan.com The "NIV" and "New International Version" are trademarks registered in the United States Patent and Trademark Office by Biblica, Inc.™ • Scripture quotations are from the ESV® Bible (The Holy Bible, English Standard Version®), copyright © 2001 by Crossway, a publishing ministry of Good News Publishers. Used by permission. All rights reserved. The ESV text may not be quoted in any publication made available to the public by a Creative Commons license. The ESV may not be translated in whole or in part into any other language. • Scripture quotations marked (NLT) are taken from the Holy Bible, New Living Translation, copyright ©1996, 2004, 2015 by Tyndale House Foundation. Used by permission of Tyndale House Publishers, Carol Stream, Illinois 60188. All rights reserved. • Scripture quotations marked (KJV) taken from the Holy Bible, King James Version, which is in the public domain. • Scripture quotations taken from the Amplified® Bible (AMP), Copyright © 2015 by The Lockman Foundation. Used by permission. lockman.org Quotations designated (NET) are from the NET Bible® copyright ©1996, 2019 by Biblical Studies Press, L.L.C. https://netbible.com All rights reserved. Scripture quoted by permission.

ISBN: 978-1-4866-2427-0
eBook ISBN: 978-1-4866-2428-7

Word Alive Press
119 De Baets Street Winnipeg, MB R2J 3R9
www.wordalivepress.ca

WORD ALIVE
—P R E S S—

Cataloguing in Publication information can be obtained from Library and Archives Canada.

To my family, to my husband
and my wonderful children, the 3JKs.
You are my world.

CONTENTS

INTRODUCTION

I am the Lord, the God of all mankind.
Is anything too hard for me?
(Jeremiah 32:27, NIV)

AS HUMANS, WE take pride in many things. We take pride in our degrees, because to some extent they open doors to success. We take pride in our families, for they provide the moral support we need and give us a good standing in society. Some take pride in their wealth, while others take pride in their physical fitness. Still others boast of their spiritual gifts.

However, Paul said that whoever wants to boast should boast in the Lord (1 Corinthians 1:31). Jeremiah also said, *"[B]ut let the one who boasts boast about this: that they have the understanding to know me, that I am the Lord, who exercises kindness, justice and righteousness on earth, for in these I delight"* (Jeremiah 9:24, NIV).

If you have God, you have everything. Christ in you is the hope of glory (Colossians 1:27). So why not boast?

As Moses said, there is no other great people whose gods are like our God. In Him, we are called great, and therefore we have reason to boast. This should be a message of pride for every believer: "I am the Lord God Almighty." It reminds us of the identity of the God in whom we believe.

But it is also a key message of my story.

In 2016, my husband and I pastored a church in Rwanda. It was part-time work for me, since I had a career as an IT specialist. On the last Sunday of July that summer, I preached the Word from Genesis 18:14. The theme was this question: "Is there anything too hard for our God?"

Surprisingly, when I next had occasion to preach, I returned to the same theme. And for the rest of the year, whenever I had the opportunity to preach, I felt the conviction of the Holy Spirit to return to this theme.

In total, I preached nine messages about how our God is all-powerful. What could be more important for believers than to know that our God is above everything, that there is nothing He cannot do, that there is no miracle He cannot perform, no disease He cannot heal, no negative circumstance He cannot undo?

What I didn't know at the time is that I was prophesying about my own life.

At the beginning of January 2017, everything I knew in life came crumbling at my feet. I was crushed by problems from all sides: career, finances, health, family, ministry, and reputation. Trouble came in every form you can imagine.

My health slowly deteriorated, and for many months the doctors unsuccessfully tried to figure out what condition I suffered from. I had no idea that I was suffering from a life-threatening illness, though it would be easily treated once diagnosed.

Unfortunately, it took time to arrive at the correct diagnosis.

I was made miserable while having to endure the advice of all the so-called spiritual Christians who told me, "Relax. Trust God. Let go of your stress. That is what's making you sick." The more I prayed, the more my problem seemed to intensify.

Then the Lord reminded me of the message I had preached the previous year. I went back to my notes and hated what I read. However, this was the start of my life-transforming journey. To grasp all the great things God had in store for me, I had to go back to His spiritual drawing board and be made anew.

Prior to that period of my life, I could easily say that I had never known a life of hardship. I was born and raised in a stable, loving family. I married into a good family. I didn't experience much in terms of lack, strife, or struggle.

It's strange to think that only after more than twenty years of salvation did I start to learn how to live by faith! There are things you can only understand when you live them for yourself. Under those circumstances, you can measure the level of trust you have in the Lord. It's not that people forget that God is all able; rather, most of the time, under the heaviness of adversity, we lose focus and need to be reminded that the God we believe in is *almighty*.

I realized that I'm not the only one who needed this reminder. Even John the Baptist, whom Jesus called the greatest prophet, was at one point shaken and requested to see Jesus for reassurance. When the messengers came to relay the message to Jesus, He didn't say, "Go and tell John that I am the Messiah." Instead He told them to recount to John how God's power is manifested through miracles.

Yes, from time to time we all need to be reminded that His name is El Shaddai.

I still haven't totally gotten out of the pit, but little by little I am climbing the ladder. All in all, one thing is sure: our God is almighty. As believers, we should never entertain a shadow of doubt that God will act on our behalf. We mustn't allow even the tiniest crack in our belief. Does a responsible parent ever fail to act according to the needs of his or her children?

God also doesn't hold anything back. He makes sure we live the best lives and become the best versions of ourselves. Of course, His ways are not our ways and His thoughts are not our thoughts. His ways of doing things may be different from what we imagine, but He always shows up. He is no respecter of persons and His miracles are not reserved for some and withheld from others. What He did for others, He will do for you too.

He is still the same forever. As we read in 1 Corinthians 2:9–10, "'What no eye has seen, what no ear has heard, and what no human mind has conceived'—the things God has prepared for those who love him…" (NIV)

x

one

HE GIVES POWER TO THE WEAK

*He gives power to the weak and strength to the
powerless. Even youths will become weak and tired,
and young men will fall in exhaustion. But those
who trust in the Lord will find new strength.
They will soar high on wings like eagles.
They will run and not grow weary.
They will walk and not faint.*
(Isaiah 40:29–31, NLT)

SOMETIMES WHEN YOU receive a revelation or word of prophecy, you feel like laughing. Sarah laughed when she was told that she would have a son, for she was well past her childbearing years (Genesis 18:9–14). In her eyes, those words sounded like a joke. Even worse, a joke in bad taste.

God's Word can be too much to bear. When Abraham received confirmation that he would have a son of promise with Sarah, he also laughed, replying to God, *"If only Ishmael might live under your blessing!"* (Genesis 17:18, NIV) In other words, "I have given up on the thought of having a child with Sarah. Let's not talk about it anymore. Ishmael will do."

But God asked them, "Is anything too hard for me? I am God Almighty. I can do all things." This is the same question He has asked throughout the history of man, and He is still asking it today.

Is there anything you think He can't do? No. Because with Him, nothing is impossible. We know this to be the absolute truth.

We must be assured that we can achieve everything God designs for us, since He is the one who does the work. If He says, "Abraham and Sarah, you will have a child of your own," then that is what will happen. If He tells a young shepherd, "You will be king over My people," that happens. If His design is for a young and unknown orphan girl to become the queen of a foreign land, that happens.

Philippians 4:13 says, *"I can do all things through Christ who strengthens me"* (NKJV). This verse is often quoted outside of its context, but it still means what it means: with Christ, we can do all things we have been called to do, regardless of our current circumstances.

When Paul wrote that scripture, he was referring to his financial conditions. He had learned to be content with little and live in abundance without feeling self-important. He wasn't crushed by anything or limited in any way. Nothing distracted him. In every way, he was able to accomplish what Christ had called him to do—not because of his strength, ability, or qualifications but because of Christ who empowered him.

The Bible says, *"Everything is possible for the one who believes"* (Mark 9:23, NIV). But what does *everything* mean? It has nothing to do with our carnal desires. The fact that you want something doesn't mean you will necessarily achieve it, even if you work hard. However, everything that comes out of the Lord's mouth for you, everything that aligns with His design for your life, is yours to possess. You can claim it whether it makes sense or not, whether people believe it or not, or whether you have what it takes to achieve it or not.

Regardless of conditions, everything is possible to we who believe what God says about us. Because it's not accomplished by our power but by God's.

Is there anything too hard for the Lord? No. But here's the catch: you must possess the master key that opens all doors. What is the master key? Believing and walking in that belief.

You Are a Mighty Man/Woman of Valour

God gives power to the weak. That doesn't only apply to those who are physically weary. It also means that He enables people to do what ordinarily they couldn't do. They soar high, achieving things they otherwise couldn't dream about.

We're all weak and unable to do things on our own. But through His power, we become mighty men and women who are able to do all those things that Christ has set for us to do. As God's children, created in His image, His power is in us. This is why the Bible calls us mighty. But we must plug into His power for our power to manifest.

It is by God's power that ordinary people from the Bible became the giants of faith who continue to inspire our lives today. Abraham and Sarah, Joseph, David, and Esther are mighty figures.

Gideon was called a mighty man of valour. Though he wasn't aware of it, he was a dormant giant. On the day when he connected with God's power through the spoken Word, it became visible that he was transformed from an ordinary person into an extraordinary one.

Now the Angel of the Lord came and sat under the terebinth tree which was in Ophrah, which belonged to Joash the Abiezrite, while his son Gideon threshed wheat in the winepress, in order to hide it from the Midianites. And the Angel of the Lord appeared to him, and said to him, **"The Lord is with you, you mighty man of valor!"**

Gideon said to Him, **"O my lord, if the Lord is with us, why then has all this happened to us?** And where are all His miracles which our fathers told us about, saying, 'Did not the Lord bring us up from Egypt?' But now the Lord has forsaken us and delivered us into the hands of the Midianites."

Then the Lord turned to him and said, **"Go in this might of yours,** and you shall save Israel from the hand of the Midianites. Have I not sent you?"

So he said to Him, "O my Lord, how can I save Israel? Indeed **my clan is the weakest in Manasseh, and I am the least in my father's house.**"

And the Lord said to him, "**Surely I will be with you,** and you shall defeat the Midianites as one man." (Judges 6:11–16, NKJV, emphasis added)

The life of Gideon teaches us an important lesson about God. Since the day of Adam and Eve, His plan for man has not changed. He wants His children to have dominion and do great things. In God's Kingdom, there is no second-class citizen. We were all created in God's image. He imprinted his spiritual DNA in us. Therefore, we are all capable.

Gideon had no idea that he was a mighty man, a man called to accomplish great things. He didn't know that he had in him the capacity to deliver the Israelites from the oppression of the Midianites. His circumstances were difficult and his reasoning logical and valid.

First, he lived in challenging times under the persecution of many enemies. He was unable to do anything about it and had to hide in order to thresh wheat so he and his family could survive.

Second, even if he wanted to do something about his situation, he didn't come from a prestigious or influential family. In fact, his clan was the poorest in the tribe of Manasseh. To make matters even worse, he was the least from his own father's house.

How could such a man dream of delivering Israel? Where would he start? Who would listen to such a person, who came from nowhere?

If we're honest, we can relate to him in many ways. How could you, an unknown son and daughter of an ordinary genealogy, dream of achieving anything great? Your hometown may be like Nazareth, a place from which nothing good could come, or Galilee, which had never produced a prophet.

Gideon had the right to question the Angel's greeting. He knew that he had no power, so he presented his case to the Angel of the Lord. The Angel didn't say, "I will give you power." Instead He told Gideon, *"Go in this might of yours"* (Judges 6:14, NKJV). He didn't need anything else; God had already deposited in him what was required for such an assignment. The rest was God's affair.

You don't need to see with your eyes to believe that you have what it takes for the assignment that's been given to you. Everything you need is already within you. When you plug into God's Word, everything becomes possible for you.

What is your story today? What is your background? Where do you come from? Who are your parents? Do you feel like you're trapped by your background or circumstances? Do you feel like you can't achieve anything?

None of these considerations has the potential to limit you, because the One who calls you is all-powerful. If need be, He will remove obstacles within you and create you anew to allow you to accomplish your destiny.

Moses's story is the proof. One day, Moses stood in front of God and said, "I can't stand before Pharaoh and deliver Israel because I don't speak properly. I stutter and you know it. I've had this problem for a long time." God answered him: *"Who has made man's mouth? Or who makes the mute, the deaf, the seeing, or the blind? Have not I, the Lord?"* (Exodus 4:11, NKJV)

In other words, God was telling him that if his mouth was dysfunctional now, He could create a new one.

There is no excuse.

A friend of mine, a pastor, was born in one of those remote rural areas where there is no power, no tap water, nothing. One day she told me, "If I had been born in Europe or America, I would have achieved many things. I would have gotten far by now." She went on and on, telling me about the schools she would have attended, the important people she would have met, and I strongly agreed with her reasoning. She was absolutely right!

However, in that same village where my friend was born, God has since raised another woman to become an international preacher. She was what one would think of as a typical peasant housewife. She couldn't read and only spoke the local language, but God has sent her out to speak to dignitaries all over the world. "I will be your mouth," He told her. That's the same thing God did for Moses. God provided this woman with an interpreter.

The woman is in her late seventies now, but she is still delivering God's message, accompanied with signs and wonders. How and where God uses us doesn't depend on how we were born and raised. It depends on the will of the One who calls us. The things we call limitations in our lives are small matters in God's eyes.

You Are Not Alone

Another lesson we learn from Gideon is that God is always with you. You are in God's plan and on His mind. Whoever you are, you are not an accident.

You might not currently see all the signs that God is with you. You might say, like Gideon, "I've heard from others that you did wonders, but why don't I see any?" You may be asking, like him, "Why do I have to grind wheat in a cave, hiding from my enemies?"

Whatever the case is for you, whatever you are facing right now, the truth is that God is with you—and if He's with you, no opposition can stop you.

God told Moses several times, "Go to Pharaoh. I will be with you." Moses kept insisting that he couldn't do it. God told him, *"I will be with your mouth and teach you what you shall say"* (Exodus 4:12, NKJV). Here is what God is saying, paraphrased: "I will turn your weakness into your strongest asset, because in that weakness My power is manifested."

It can be very difficult to believe that God is with you when your life seems to be going in the wrong direction. Prayers aren't answered and you can't feel the presence of God. But God is not to be felt; He is to be believed and trusted. If He allows you to feel His presence, you are lucky. Rejoice and praise Him! If you don't feel Him, you are still lucky. Rejoice and praise Him still, because He is always there.

Cultivate your faith and nurture it by telling yourself over and over that He will never leave you or abandon you (Hebrews 13:5). Tell yourself that He is faithful (2 Thessalonians 3:3). Receive every single word of promise with faith and let it be your source of strength.

God always confirms His plan with us with reassuring promises. He knows that we are weak and don't fully grasp His intentions. That's why He says, "Have I not sent you?"

If you feel like doubting, ask for a sign. He is not offended when we ask for reassurance that He is with us in our endeavours.

Unleash God's Power in You

The God who is almighty intends to do mighty things with you, but you must do something in order to connect with that power.

Though Gideon was a mighty man of God, he needed to do a few things to allow the might in him to become operational. God appeared to him at night and revealed how he could put all things in order:

> Now it came to pass the same night that the Lord said to him, "Take your father's young bull, the second bull of seven years old, and tear down the altar of Baal that your father has, and cut down the wooden image that is beside it; and build an altar to the Lord your God on top of this rock in the proper arrangement, and take the second bull and offer a burnt sacrifice with the wood of the image which you shall cut down." (Judges 6:25–26, NKJV)

These verses highlight two essential tasks which should be undertaken in order to unleash the power of God in you.

First, God wants you to tear down the altar of Baal and the wooden image beside it (which is also known as the pole of Ashera). This means turning your back on other gods and focusing only on the one true God as your source of salvation and help. For some, other gods can be the source of one's wealth, education, family and friends, etc. When we still have other options, God doesn't manifest. He is not meant to be *an* option, but *the* option. Once we learn that God is the only Helper to whom we can run, and once we align our actions to this truth, God's power will manifest in our lives.

Second, the Lord requires that we build an altar to Him. The altar represents our relationship with God. We can't destroy our communion with false gods without replacing it with fellowship with the true God. Jesus illustrated this principle in Matthew 12:43–45:

When an unclean spirit goes out of a man, he goes through dry places, seeking rest, and finds none. Then he says, "I will return to my house from which I came." And when he comes, he finds it empty, swept, and put in order. Then he goes and takes with him seven other spirits more wicked than himself, and they enter and dwell there; and the last state of that man is worse than the first. So shall it also be with this wicked generation. (NKJV).

Like it or not, if God isn't the one who occupies your heart. If Jesus isn't your master, then someone else is—Satan. If you kick out Satan, make sure to surrender to the Lord.

Build an Altar to God

In Genesis 35, God called Jacob to Bethel, which means the "house of God," and instructed him to build an altar there and dwell there. Scripture says,

Then God said to Jacob, "Arise, go up to Bethel and dwell there; and make an altar there to God, who appeared to you when you fled from the face of Esau your brother."

And Jacob said to his household and to all who were with him, "Put away the foreign gods that are among you, purify yourselves, and change your garments. Then let us arise and go up to Bethel; and I will make an altar there to God, who answered me in the day of my distress and has been with me in the way which I have gone." (Genesis 35:1–3, NKJV)

The fellowship that activates the power within us requires that we live and remain in the house of God, continually beholding His presence.

When God gave the promise to Abraham to possess the land, he went all over the country establishing altars (Genesis 12:6–8). Abraham's act was a sign of bringing God's presence into the land. We must take God wherever we go. We must ensure that God is part of what we do by deliberately involving Him in our daily lives, not just calling Him when things are difficult. This requires us to lead a life of praise and worship in holiness.

The altar is where praise and worship are rendered to God. In the Old Testament, the Israelites would bring peace offerings to be burned on the altar; these were thanksgiving offerings. There is no praise or worship if we aren't grateful to God for all that He has done in our lives. A heart of praise and worship draws near to God and opens doors to the outpouring of His power.

In the Old Testament, burnt offerings were sacrificed on the altar for the people to atone for their sins. The fellowship with God we're talking about is manifested through a repentant heart. It is impossible to see God when we harbour sin in our lives. Repentance and holiness open our hearts to see God (Hebrews 12:14).

Separate Yourself

The Lord had one final requirement before he could elevate Gideon to the position He had designed for him.

First, he had to separate from the fearful. The Bible says,

> The Lord said to Gideon, "The people with you are too many for me to give the Midianites into their hand, lest Israel boast over me, saying, 'My own hand has saved me.' Now therefore proclaim in the ears of the people, saying, **'Whoever is fearful and trembling, let him return home** and hurry away from Mount Gilead.'" **Then 22,000 of the people returned, and 10,000 remained.** (Judges 7:2–3, ESV, emphasis added)

To achieve your great potential, you must pay attention to the people you walk with. Separate yourself from the fearful, the doubters, and the mockers. Such people walk by sight and not by faith. You will be tempted and led to do as they do. The rabble who followed the Israelites when God delivered them from Egypt contributed a lot to Israel's decision to rebel against God and thus remain in the wilderness for forty years (Numbers 11:4). Fear and unbelief are contagious. Do not associate yourself with them.

Gideon also had to part ways with another group: those who had failed God's test. It is not clear what that test accounted for, but for God it meant something. Scripture states,

> And the Lord said to Gideon, "The people are still too many. Take them down to the water, and I will test them for you there, and anyone of whom I say to you, 'This one shall go with you,' shall go with you, and anyone of whom I say to you, 'This one shall not go with you,' shall not go." (Judges 7:4, ESV)

Wherever you are and whatever you are striving to achieve, if God tells you, "Do not go with someone," then don't go with them—even if they are family—for they are not meant to be with you on your journey, for reasons known only to God.

Lot wasn't supposed to be part of Abraham's calling, but Abraham decided to include him. However, because that relationship wasn't meant to be, they couldn't stay together. Their separation was rough. They could have spared themselves much heartache had they evolved separately.

Share in the Glory of the Master

For those who achieve their God-given mission, whether small or big, there is only one reward: *"Well done, good and faithful servant… Enter into the joy of your master"* (Matthew 25:21, ESV). They get to share in the glory of their Master.

After you've torn apart the altar of Baal and Ashera, build an altar to the Lord and separate yourself from negative influences. Then you will be ready to receive God's power, which will make all things possible for you. As you submit your life to do His will, God allows you to share in His fame and test the glory that awaits those who accomplish what they were designed for.

In the time of Gideon, the battle cry became, *"A sword for the Lord and for Gideon!"* (Judges 7:20, NIV) This is how one's name becomes great. It may not be great in the eyes of the people, but certainly in the eye of the One who has chosen you. Becoming famous is not God's ultimate goal for you, though, nor should it be your own. It happens as a consequence of obeying God and allowing Him to work through you according to His purpose.

You have been called to accomplish great things that impact humanity. Your mission may be carried out in secret, only known to you and God, or in public for everyone to see. It may look as small as praying for your spouse, raising godly children, and serving your master well. Or it may look as big as saving your country, like Gideon, or being the father and mother of many nations, like Abraham and Sarah, or even changing nations, like Paul.

Though this chapter primarily focuses on those who have been called for spectacular achievement, no one can accomplish anything without God. No matter how big or impossible it may be to walk in God's calling for you, even if it makes you laugh in unbelief as with Abraham and Sarah, it will happen because God gives His people the knowledge and ability they need, regardless of their external circumstances.

You have been set aside for great work. You are a mighty man or woman of power, destined to accomplish that which you have been called to do. Don't hesitate to step into your destiny with full confidence in His capacity, not your own. Yes, you can and will prevail through Christ who gives you the power, for nothing is impossible to Him.

Just remember: the master key that opens every door is this word—*believe*.

HE RAISES FROM THE ASHES

He raises the poor from the dust and lifts
the needy from the ash heap…
(Psalm 113:7, NIV)

PEOPLE SAY THAT life is unfair. Can we say that too, as Christians? Spiritually speaking, life is good because it is a gift from God. But it can also be hard and push you into a state of extreme brokenness— crushed, grinded down, and torn into thousands of pieces.

I tend to believe that we live the majority of our lives here on the earth in hardship, fighting to survive. As one man of God once told me, most of the time we are more broken than whole, humanly speaking.

Jacob the patriarch held the same view. When Pharoah asked him how old he was, he replied, *"My years have been few and difficult…"* (Genesis 47:9, NIV) Inspired by the Spirit of God, Moses also wrote, *"Our days may come to seventy years, or eighty, if our strength endures; yet the best of them are but trouble and sorrow, for they quickly pass, and we fly away"* (Psalm 90:10, NIV).

In light of what the Scriptures state, it would not be carnal to say that life is hard. We encounter crushing disappointment and pain lies in every corner of our short lives.

When crushed down, one has two options: to stay down and give up or to rise, remove the dust, and continue the journey. However, there are situations when you can't get up on your own, even if you want it with all your heart and try with all your strength.

Glory be to our God, who can do all things, because such situations are nothing in His eyes. The good news is that no matter how far one may go, or how deep one may sink, there is always the possibility of rising back up if you are willing to fight and work with God. His arm is long enough to reach into any bottomless pit.

It has been said that however long is the night, the dawn will break; the sun always rises in the morning. Psalm 30:5 also adds that *"weeping may endure for a night, but joy cometh in the morning"* (KJV). Life is a cycle. Our situations won't always be bad, nor will they always be good. But we know this for sure: even if you have been ruined and left in a pile of ash, God can and will lift you up.

When I think of total ruin, two stories come to mind to illustrate the restorative power of God. I am Rwandan to the core, and obviously I am proud of my country. That said, I am awed to contemplate what has God has done for us. Meditating on His work on our behalf makes me realize over and over again how great He is.

In 1994, Rwanda experienced one of the worst human tragedies in history: the genocide against the Tutsi. More than one million people perished in a period of one hundred days. On average, ten thousand people were killed every day in a country with a population below ten million at the time. Think upon how extreme this atrocity was! Can you imagine anything worse? The people killed their countrymen, relatives, and neighbours to extermination.

Figuratively speaking, Rwanda was a heap of ashes. No one gave a second thought to its survival. It was thought that recovery was impossible, that the country would become a failed state. Yet with God, the country managed to pull itself out of the pit, and after only twenty-nine years Rwanda is now one of the most stable and thriving countries in the world.

Pompeii is another story. This city in southern Italy was destroyed in 79 A.D. and buried under four to six metres of volcanic ash after the eruption of Mount Vesuvius. Pompeii had been a thriving Roman city, but the eruption killed almost all its inhabitants and the city was entirely lost, so much so that its ruins weren't rediscovered until the last decade of the sixteenth century. For almost fifteen centuries, the city was forgotten. No one believed it could ever live again after such a long period of time.

That area is now one of the beautiful sites in Italy, drawing approximately two and a half million visitors every year. Today Pompeii is recorded as a UNESCO World Heritage Site.

Can Dry Bones Live Again?

These two stories are comparable to the story of the dry bones we read in Ezekiel 37. There is no life left in a dry bone. In this story, God asked the prophet Ezekiel a very important question: can dry bones live again?

> The hand of the Lord came upon me and brought me out in the Spirit of the Lord, and set me down in the midst of the valley; and it was full of bones. Then He caused me to pass by them all around, and behold, there were very many in the open valley; and indeed they were very dry. And He said to me, "Son of man, can these bones live?"
>
> So I answered, "O Lord God, You know."
>
> Again He said to me, "Prophesy to these bones, and say to them, 'O dry bones, hear the word of the Lord! Thus says the Lord God to these bones: "Surely I will cause breath to enter into you, and you shall live. I will put sinews on you and bring flesh upon you, cover you with skin and put breath in you; **and you shall live. Then you shall know that I am the Lord**."'" (Ezekiel 37:1–6, NKJV, emphasis added)

Yes, dry bones can live again. Like Ezekiel, you may not be sure of the answer. The prophet didn't want to commit himself. But by the Word of God, a word of prophecy, it is confirmed that, yes, dry bones can live.

Notice that these were the bones of people who had been dead for a long time by the time God talked to the prophet! Your figurative dry bones can also live. God's Word can and will give life to that which has seemingly died in your life—and you and the people around you shall know that the Lord is God and that the hand of God has accomplished it.

He Raises the Poor from the Dust

Does your life look like Pompeii now? Do you feel like you're six feet under? Do you feel abandoned and forgotten, buried under the pressure of life, what Moses called trouble and sorrow? Has everyone abandoned you, as they did my country?

God is still able to pull you out of the mess. You may feel crushed to the point of becoming dust. You may wonder how God will be able to patch you up again and make you whole. But He can and He will. By the Spirit of the Lord, all your scattered pieces will be brought together again.

You may tell me, "Wait here. You don't know my story. I'm too damaged to be patched up." You're right in that I don't know your story, but I know all about the God in whom we believe. He will take your dust and create you afresh, like He did in Eden. His Spirit will give you life. This scripture will become your new story: *"Then the Lord God formed a man from the dust of the ground and breathed into his nostrils the breath of life, and the man became a living being"* (Genesis 2:7, NIV).

The Bible also says, *"He raises the poor from the dust and lifts the beggar from the ash heap, to set them among princes and make them inherit the throne of glory"* (1 Samuel 2:8, NKJV). There is no position so low that the hand of the Lord will not reach down to touch you. And there is no position so high that the Lord is unable to take you there. He won't only raise you; He will also elevate you and give you honour and prominence.

The dry bones of Ezekiel didn't just live again. They became a vast army! In the same way, God raised Rwanda, just as He did Pompeii, for there is nothing too hard for him. To those who believe, everything is possible. The combination of these two powerful biblical truths produces miracles beyond human understanding.

If God has done this for others, He will also do it for you. He is no respecter of person. When the time is right, His hand will do it.

Promise of Restoration

Regardless of the reason your life became broken, the Lord has given us a promise of restoration. Whether you're the victim of a natural disaster or villains who have agreed to be used for evil, whether you're suffering from your own mistakes, Jesus is telling you this:

> The Spirit of the Sovereign Lord is on me, because the Lord has anointed me to proclaim good news to the poor. He has sent me to bind up the brokenhearted, to proclaim freedom for the captives and release from darkness for the prisoners… (Isaiah 61:1 NIV)

This is the reason Jesus came, not only to reconcile us with the Father through His death and resurrection but also to show us that God is concerned by our physical and emotional needs. There is still hope. Even if a tree is cut down, it will sprout again and its new shoots will not fail (Job 14:7).

No amount of external hardship will be able to kill you, because though housed in a body you are a spirit. The body can succumb, but the spirit does not; it comes from God. Unless you give up, your spirit will keep fighting to rise. And the more pressure your spirit receives, the more glorious your life will be when God fulfills the promise of Isaiah 61:1 in your life.

Consider a spring in the realm physics. The more you try to hold it down, the higher it will jump when the force is released.

Is there anyone under the sun who was hit like Job? He is the perfect representation of the needy sitting in ashes. He lost everything and his friends turned their backs on him, accusing him of lying and hiding unconfessed sin. His wife, who was supposed to be the source of moral support, told him, "Just give up. Stop fighting and die."

Thank God that Job did not give up! Instead he sprang forth with an incredible promotion and rose twice as high. He gained twice as much in terms of possession, honour, glory, and every other respect you can imagine.

Make Gains from Your Pain

Pain doesn't make sense. Why do we have to suffer?

Unfortunately, pain is part of the deal. As long as the world remains under the devil's influence, nothing can be done about this. Yet when faced with extreme challenges, people ask many questions: why me, why now, what did I do? Sometimes they even question God's fairness.

However, the truth is that you are not alone. Everyone suffers. If others were to open their hearts to you, you would be shocked to know how much hardship they deal with. Evil is everywhere; believers and unbelievers suffer the same.

But people overcome everyday too. Therefore, be encouraged by those who overcame before you. Know this: in the world where Jesus is King, nothing is wasted. Even your pain, in God's hand, is a powerful tool for you and others who come into contact with you. Build from the stones that life throws at you and make gains from bad experiences, opposition, and failure. Let them become your lesson books. With God, you will rise again.

I once read a fictional story on the internet that really inspired me. There was a farmer who owned a horse. One day, the horse fell in a deep pit and the farmer was incapable of pulling it out. The horse cried out in agony from deep in the pit.

The farmer, unable to bear the painful weeping, decided to bury the animal to ease its pain. He started throwing dust in the pit.

At the first shovelful, though, the horse, realizing what was happening, cried even more.

After some time, the noise ceased and the farmer thought the horse had died. He leaned down over the opening of the pit to see into the depths—only to be startled by what he saw.

The horse had received a life-changing revelation! It had been able to use the dust to emerge out of the pit. With each shovelful of dust, the horse shook it and stepped onto it.

The farmer was so happy about the discovery that he went to the neighbours and called as many as possible to help him throw more shovelfuls of dust in the pit. And in no time, the horse was out!

Happy ending, right?

Let us learn from the horse. Shake the dust thrown at you and trample it under your feet. I know it's easier said than done. Unfortunately, we have only two alternatives: step on the dust and rise, or accept to be buried under it and die.

Let adversity sharpen your mind. Let the fight strengthen your muscles. Let deception raise your desire for self-reliance. Let failure open your eyes to other options. Shake the dust loose, for it is your ladder to climb out.

I once fell in a pit of life too. At one time, I went downhill and reached a point where I felt I couldn't sink any lower. I hit the bottom of a deep hole. While down there, I pictured Satan looking down on me and saying, like Joseph's brothers, "Let's see what will become of your dreams."

Honestly, I didn't want to do anything. It was as if I had resigned myself to enduring the devil's mockery.

Then I realized that I had only two options. I could stay down, feeling sorry for myself, or I could swallow my humiliation, pain, and discouragement and rise. I could give glory to the devil or give glory to God, but not both.

I chose God. I revived my dreams and became more ambitious. With God, I will always be on the right track.

Hannah, the mother of the prophet Samuel, declared herself to be barren. For a woman, not being able to conceive and bear children is the worst emotional pain she can endure. It is humiliating and denigrating. In Hannah's case, there was the additional torment of her rival, who had children.

Her words, recorded in 1 Samuel 2:1–8, were the expression of her soul. She felt at the lowest level possible, like a destitute woman sitting amidst ashes.

However, she took the pain, humiliation, and abuse she suffered and transformed it into power, giving her the resolve to pray and seek God until she managed to climb out of her pit. The more insults she received, the more she prayed, and God heard her prayers. At last God elevated her and gave her a son who was great in the land.

This is what the Lord does. As long as there is breath in you, God can take you to the highest level, for *"even a live dog is better off than a dead lion!"* (Ecclesiasts 9:4, NIV)

HE WORKS EVEN AFTER FOUR DAYS

*On his arrival, Jesus found that Lazarus had already
been in the tomb for four days.*
(John 11:17, NIV)

IS GOD EVER late? It may seem as though God was late in the case of
Abraham, seeing as Sarah's biological clock had seemingly stopped
ticking! The Bible says that *"it ceased to be with Sarah after the
manner of women"* (Genesis 18:11, KJV).

In John 11, God also seemed to be late in the case of Lazarus.
We read that *"Lazarus had already been in the tomb for four days"*
(John 11:17, NIV).

According to our schedule, God seems to be late most of the
time, but the truth is that He is never late according to His timing and
infinite wisdom.

Lazarus's story is well known. This guy was not an ordinary man;
he and his sisters were Jesus's friends. Throughout the life of Jesus on
the earth, not many people were referred to as His friends!

One day Lazarus fell sick to the point of death and his sisters
sent a word to their Friend, who could heal him. They thought, since
He loved them, that he would come as soon as He heard the news.
It would be a priority.

However, they were wrong. Jesus did not come right away.

Sometimes, in our deepest hour of need, God decides to wait.
Very weird. How can one's Friend decide to delay when He knows
very well that He's desperately needed?

In this case, Jesus delayed two days, which resulted in Him arriving four days late. By the time He arrived, Lazarus had already died.

In our walk with God, the truth is that it is rare that He answers our prayer right away. There is always a time of waiting. I call this period "the four days," regardless of how long it lasts. It is a very difficult time because our human nature doesn't like to wait. Patience is not in our DNA. If you are suffering and struggling, the more time passes, the more it hurts; the pain doesn't get any better even if you are patient.

Most of the time, the situation is bearable initially. We still hope that God will intervene. We keep telling our souls, "Trust in the Lord. He will show up for you."

But as the days pass, the situation deteriorates and becomes progressively unbearable to the point that all hope seems lost. The situation has gone from bad to worse, and then from worse to the irreversible.

Instead of receiving your answer, you feel like you're falling into a pit. Then you hit rock bottom and can't sink any further. It's too late; the Lord is late.

Like Mary and Martha told Jesus, if He had shown up on time, things would not have reached the point of no return. Initially Lazarus had been sick. Nothing to worry about. He would get better. Then he was very sick, and finally he died, was buried, and started decomposing.

Why does Jesus make us wait? Only He knows. But there are at least three important things that happen during this period.

God Tests Your Heart

During the time of waiting, the condition of your heart is exposed. Many things in your heart remain hidden until something like a tsunami shakes it. As Jeremiah 17:9 tells us, *"The heart is deceitful above all things and beyond cure. Who can understand it?"* (NIV)

Martha's statements to Jesus show her confusion. She said, *"If you had been here, my brother would not have died. But I know that even now God will give you whatever you ask"* (John 11:21–22, NIV). My simple understanding of her words is that she believed, that even after her brother's death, that Jesus could resurrect him, if He asked His Father. A moment later, she said, *"I know he will rise again in the resurrection at the last day"* (John 11:24, NIV).

So did Martha believe that Jesus could do it, or didn't she? I'm sure that she herself didn't recognize her own conflicting thoughts. She knew Jesus could raise the dead, since He had already raised the son of the widow of Nain and the daughter of Jairus. Everyone knew. But the shock of her brother's death could have made her question how far her faith in the Lord could go. Perhaps she thought, *He can raise someone who has just died, but not one who is already in the tomb for four days.*

In Deuteronomy 8, God tells the people of Israel that their forty years of waiting in the wilderness were meant to test them and see if they were ready to obey Him in all His ways:

Remember how the Lord your God led you all the way in the wilderness these forty years, to humble and test you in order to know what was in your heart, whether or not you would keep his commands. (Deuteronomy 8:2. NIV)

The more pressure is put on you, the more the true nature of your heart is revealed. You discover tendencies, emotions, and even sins that you were never aware were hidden there. The recognition of hidden sin and flaws allows God to work in you and change your life completely. Unless a person is shaken and emptied from vessel to vessel, they can never change (Jeremiah 48:11).

God's test of waiting produces patience in us, a virtue without which we can't operate as mature Christians. Without patience, we behave like spoiled children, always wailing for this and that.

Patience teaches and trains us to endure. The human spirit is strong because it comes from God. However, the mind and the will are weak; they need to be strengthened through testing. James says,

> My brethren, count it all joy when you fall into various trials, knowing that the testing of your faith produces patience. But let patience have its perfect work, that you may be perfect and complete, lacking nothing. (James 1:2–4, NKJV)

When patience has produced its fruits, one can say, like David, *"My flesh and my heart fail, but God is the strength of my heart and my portion forever"* (Psalms 73:26, NKJV).

God Reveals People's Hearts

The figurative four days of waiting is the period during which God reveals people's hearts. Why is that important? Because you are on a journey of transformation. When God appears after the four days, you will be someone new, called for new things and called to walk and work with new people.

The Bible says, *"Do two walk together unless they have agreed to do so?"* (Amos 3:3, NIV) You can only agree with someone if you have the same priorities, understandings, and views. That's why God wants you to be aware of who you walk with.

You will discover three types of people: those who mock, those who feel sorry for your situation, and those who comfort and encourage you to rise and do something. You will discover true friends and the hypocrites who only stay with you as long as it profits them.

Not everyone will be on your side, no matter how good you are to them. Even if you were to give your life to people, many wouldn't recognize your sacrifice. Even God, the Creator of all, doesn't have everyone on His side! So don't take it to heart when you realize that the majority of those around you are mockers.

During your days of waiting, God will reveal to you these mockers, who are quick to say, "Where is your God? You trusted Him so much. Why can't He rescue you? If He really loved you, He should have helped you by now. Curse Him and die."

Mockers were present at Lazarus's tomb. Instead of comforting Mary and Martha, they said, *"Could not he who opened the eyes of the blind man have kept this man from dying?"* (John 11:37, NIV)

I think Job's three friends were mockers too. They didn't offer any comfort. Instead they made his misery worse while accusing him of sin.

You will never know these people unless their hearts are exposed.

You will also discover the sympathizers, those who feel sorry for you but nothing more. There were some sympathizers at Lazarus's tomb. When they saw Jesus crying, they said, *"See how he loved him!"* (John 11:36, NIV)

These people may have sympathy for what you're going through, but they aren't willing to suffer with you. They are like Orpah, willing to go with you a few miles but not escort you all the way; they have their own families and their own businesses. They are nice people who aren't meant to walk with you for the particular season of testing. They are like Elkanah, blowing on your wound and giving you a massage while never pushing you to rise and do something. They will not go with you to the temple when you call upon your God and plead for a miracle.

Finally, God allows you to know your comrades, companions, and comforters. These are the people who stayed with Mary and Martha in their home and comforted them, following them wherever they went so the sisters wouldn't be left alone. They knew the women needed consolation and were ready to give it to them (John 11:31).

These people are like Ruth, angels whom God has placed at your side to help you until you're back on your feet again. They are there to pray with you, encourage you, and even push you if need be. They stick with you and help at the risk of incurring the anger of the higher-ups. They may not be part of your calling, but you can count on them always rooting for you.

God Reveals Himself

Most importantly, in these days of waiting you will discover who Jesus really is. He wants to reveal Himself to you, so you can know how powerful and capable He is.

Jesus was pleased that Lazarus died when He wasn't there, because He wanted His disciples to know Him in another dimension. When it was time for Jesus to announce to His disciples that Lazarus was dead, He said, *"Lazarus is dead, and for your sake I am glad I was not there, so that you may believe. But let us go to him"* (John 11:14–15, NIV).

At the tomb, before He called Lazarus out, He prayed to the Father: *"Father, I thank you that you have heard me. I knew that you always hear me, but I said this for the benefit of the people standing here, that they may believe that you sent me"* (John 11:41–42, NIV). Jesus had said that Lazarus's sickness wouldn't kill him and would showcase the glory of the Father and the Son. Even though he ended up dying, in God's eye it was not death, but rather a means of revealing His nature to His disciples.

Paul said, *"I want to know Christ—yes, to know the power of his resurrection and participation in his sufferings, becoming like him in his death…"* (Philippians 3:10, NIV) I am sure that every Christian prays like Paul: "I want to know You, Lord." However, there is a price to knowing Him. If Jesus hadn't delayed four days, Mary and Martha would not have known Him. His disciples, the Jews, the Pharisees, and the priests would not have known Him.

Despite the pain and agony, the Lord allows this time of waiting so that at the end you will say, like Job, *"My ears had heard of you but now my eyes have seen you"* (Job 42:5, NIV). You will no longer speak about the God you have heard but of the God you have seen.

God Seen in Action

The text of 2 Kings 6:24–33 and 2 Kings 7:1–16 reveals to us a manifestation of God working after the period of waiting, after things have gone from bad to worse and from worse to the point of no return.

Here we read the story of Samaria in the times of the prophet Elisha. The famine was raging in the city. That was bad enough, but unfortunately Samaria was also under siege. The people were prisoners in their own homes; there was no free movement within the city. The people couldn't go out to plough their fields or find food in neighbouring counties.

The people were already in the midst of a bad famine, but the situation worsened to the point that they started to eat donkeys' heads and doves' droppings. Their living conditions eventually reached the seemingly irreversible state at which women had to resort to eating their own children. This really does sounds like a point of no return!

Fortunately, in God's eyes, it was not yet the end. Instead it was the beginning of a great story, a new chapter in which God would record extraordinary miracles to be read by everyone. God was showing a small part of His power through a great deliverance. The city was delivered from the great army that marched against it—delivered by four lepers. This led to a spectacular turn of events wherein the people woke up in hunger and went to sleep in plenty.

Do you think such miracles only happened in biblical times? If so, you are very wrong. Miracles still happen today, mind-blowing miracles akin to those of the Old and New Testaments—because Jesus Christ is the same yesterday, today, and tomorrow.

When my younger sister was twenty-one years old, she was diagnosed with a tumour in one of her ovaries. There was no way of saving it, so the ovary was removed along with the tumour.

The doctors then told her and my parents that even the other ovary was sick. However, they didn't want to remove it right away because they wanted to give her the chance to have children. But she would have to marry and have children in the next two years, otherwise she would never have them.

Unfortunately, this period of time passed without her getting married.

God was nonetheless about to write a new chapter in her life. She married six years later, and although she didn't get pregnant right away she prayed all kinds of prayers. God kept telling her and her husband that they would have children, despite the doctors who kept saying it was impossible. In fact, the doctors insisted on removing her remaining ovary before it turned cancerous.

After five years of marriage, she became pregnant. She and her husband went on to have three beautiful and healthy children.

But that is not the whole story.

When they went to the gynaecologist to confirm the first pregnancy, the doctor said, "I see two normal ovaries!"

What?

"Please check again," they said.

The doctor checked again and confirmed it.

I can understand the sick ovary being healed, but it's almost too much, even now, to believe that she also grew a new one!

Worth the Trouble

We read in Haggai 2:9, *"'The glory of this present house will be greater than the glory of the former house,' says the Lord Almighty. 'And in this place I will grant peace,' declares the Lord Almighty"* (NIV). These words were spoken by the Lord through the prophets during the rebuilding of Solomon's temple, which had been destroyed seventy years before.

The elders who still remembered the first temple cried with all kinds of emotion from nostalgia to gratitude (Ezra 3:12–13). They weren't sure whether the new build would match the splendour of the first, even though God had told them that the later temple would be even more glorious.

This prophecy also pertains to the Church, that it would also surpass Solomon's temple in beauty and glory. In the same way, as the temple of the Holy Spirit, you will receive greater glory and honour when the Lord is done rebuilding you, because Jesus is glorified through His Church.

My sister's life changed completely after she had her first child. She was already a servant of God, but her ministry was elevated to a new level, much higher than she could have ever imagined.

After his resurrection, Lazarus's life and glory also far surpassed anything from before. The Bible tells us that people came from all over to see Lazarus, whom Jesus had raised from the dead: *"Meanwhile a large crowd of Jews found out that Jesus was there and came, not only because of him but also to see Lazarus, whom he had raised from the dead"* (John 12:9, NIV). Lazarus, who had only been known in his small village of Bethany, became a threat to the Pharisees, all because Jesus had delayed His intervention by four days.

I'm not sure if Lazarus and his sisters would have chosen to go through the same process again, but if we put the emotions aside we can see that it was well worth it!

Wait on the Lord with patience, for He will certainly show up: *"Indeed, none of those who [expectantly] wait for You will be ashamed; those who turn away from what is right and deal treacherously without cause will be ashamed (humiliated, embarrassed)"* (Psalms 25:3, AMP).

HE IS MIGHTY TO DELIVER

The Lord your God is in your midst; he is a warrior
who can deliver. He takes great delight in you; he
renews you by his love; he shouts for joy over you.
(Zephaniah 3:17, NET)

FREEDOM IS ONE of the ultimate values for mankind. This includes the freedom to choose, to speak, to live on one's own terms, and to love and be loved. Oppression of any kind that strips people of their freedom is a great tragedy because it deprives men of their dignity.

Freedom is a right, not a privilege. Unfortunately, at times the oppressor is so powerful that we can't set ourselves free despite all our efforts.

The book of Exodus is an account of God delivering His people from Egypt. In that time, Egypt could have been referred to as the most powerful nation in the world. They had chariots, warhorses, wealth, and advanced technology. Egypt was a superpower and Israel was a helpless and weak people who had been enslaved for more than four hundred years.

How could Israel break free from the Egyptians' grip? It was like a lamb caught between the fangs of a lion; the only thing awaiting it was death.

However, there is good news for the oppressed. God is powerful to deliver us from any kind of oppression, challenge, barrier, or obstacle that blocks our way.

God compared the oppression of Israel in Egypt to an iron-smelting furnace (Jeremiah 11:4). We don't need to know how hot a furnace is to know that it was too hot for Israel. The situation was hopeless. Even when they tried talking Pharaoh into letting them go, he oppressed them further.

I can imagine that in the evening the elders told the younger, "You know, we have a country of our own, a land flowing with milk and honey, but we don't know how to break free from the Egyptians' clutch and live like normal people."

So why did God let these things happen? The reason is always a bitter pill to swallow—salvation is dependent on God's timing.

When it was time, God deployed His arsenal of spiritual weapons against Egypt until the Egyptians urged Israel to go. Scripture says that God Himself kept vigil to bring His children out. Israel was set free in a spectacular way, after plundering its enemies. They came out of that land with riches under the mighty hand of their God.

This was the miracle of deliverance.

An Image of Salvation

The Lord told Moses, *"Now you will see what I will do to Pharaoh: Because of my mighty hand he will let them go..."* (Exodus 6:1, NIV) And He indeed showed the power of His mighty hand.

God's miracles to set Israel free were all one of a kind. Splitting the Red Sea? One of a kind. Feeding the people with heavenly food? One of a kind. Drinking from the rock? One of a kind. All these miracles were mind-blowing because they were a reflection of the deliverance God had long planned—a deliverance from the kingdom of Satan.

As Christians, when we speak of Egypt we refer to life before salvation. Moses was an image of Christ, according to what we read in Deuteronomy 18:15.

For four hundred years, Egypt oppressed the children of God—until God sent Moses. For four thousand years, the world endured the devil's reign of terror—until God sent Jesus. With a mighty hand and spectacular miracles, He rescued us from the dominion of darkness and brought us into the Kingdom of His beloved Son (Colossians 1:13).

God explained His deliverance to Moses:

Therefore, say to the Israelites: 'I am the Lord, and I will bring you out from under the yoke of the Egyptians. I will free you from being slaves to them, and I will redeem you with an outstretched arm and with mighty acts of judgment. I will take you as my own people, and I will be your God. Then you will know that I am the Lord your God, who brought you out from under the yoke of the Egyptians. (Exodus 6:6–7, NIV)

This act of redemption required God's mighty hand through the manifestation of His power. By that mighty hand, God has saved us from the kingdom of Satan, after stripping him of all authority. Jesus disarmed Satan's power and authority, making a public spectacle of them by triumphing over them on the cross (Colossians 2:15).

This is the most important miracle in a person's life—being delivered from the authority of Satan and transported into the Kingdom of the Son, a people belonging to God. It is the greatest thing God can do to a man because it opens the door to heaven and gives us an identity as children of God.

God's miracle of deliverance is final. Moses told Israel, *"The Egyptians you see today you will never see again"* (Exodus 14:13, NIV). And never again did Egypt oppress Israel while they were obedient and living in the land of the promise.

No power in heaven, on earth, or in hell will ever be able to take away your identity as a child of God, unless you alone decide so. That was God's promise then and it still stands today.

Saved to Serve

God did not just save Israel so they could peacefully settle in the land of Canaan. He saved them so they could serve His purpose. He sent Moses to Pharaoh with a clear message: to set Israel free so they could hold a festival for God, worshiping and serving Him.

> And the Lord spoke to Moses, "Go to Pharaoh and say to him, 'Thus says the Lord: "Let My people go, that they may serve Me."'" (Exodus 8:1, NKJV)

From the time of the fall of man, God had a plan to save humanity through Israel. That was God's purpose for the nation of Israel. After He saved them from the Egyptians, He made a covenant with them:

> Then the Lord said: "I am making a covenant with you. Before all your people I will do wonders never before done in any nation in all the world. The people you live among will see how awesome is the work that I, the Lord, will do for you. (Exodus 34:10, NIV)

This is also a message to the Church, the spiritual Israel who God redeemed through the blood of the Lamb. In the same manner that He delivered Israel for a purpose, we have been delivered to proclaim the good news of the Gospel. We have been chosen to be instruments of God to bring salvation to those who perish.

Here is the command Jesus gave to His disciples just before He ascended to heaven:

> And He said to them, "Go into all the world and preach the gospel to every creature. He who believes and is baptized will be saved; but he who does not believe will be condemned. And these signs will follow those who believe: In My name

they will cast out demons; they will speak with new tongues;
they will take up serpents; and if they drink anything deadly,
it will by no means hurt them; they will lay hands on the sick,
and they will recover." (Mark 16:15–18, NKJV)

The same covenant of miracles that God made with Israel as they came out of Egypt is the one He has made with the Church. Miracles must be part of the Church's life, and these will be the kind of miracles that cause the devil's magicians and sorcerers to say, "Only the finger of the Lord can do this!"

If such miracles aren't present, it is time to rise as believers and claim them. This is our right as part of Jesus's promise, for He doesn't only deliver; He also takes delight in His people. He is pleased to give us the Kingdom and dominion while we are still here on the earth (Luke 12:32).

Anointed to Deliver

Deliverance was at the heart of Jesus's ministry. In His first message in the synagogue, He told those who were present,

The Spirit of the Lord is on me, because he has anointed
me to proclaim good news to the poor. He has sent me to
proclaim freedom for the prisoners and recovery of sight for
the blind, to set the oppressed free… (Luke 4:18, NIV)

Twice in this one verse, He talks about the meaning of deliverance: to proclaim freedom and set people free.

Yes, Jesus is concerned with your freedom. Salvation is your first step in gaining freedom. But this is just the first step. You need to gain your total deliverance because the devil, who was your master, is a mighty ruler—although not almighty. The same way Pharaoh set out to bring Israel back, Satan will not sit back and let you go without a fight. He wants to keep a leash on you. He will say, "Go, but don't go far. Go, but leave your children here. Go, but leave your wealth here." You have to go all the way with all that is yours—your health, wealth, family, and all—so you can freely serve the Lord.

Some will tell you that you are delivered when you believe in your heart and confess with your mouth that Jesus is Lord. You are saved at that point, but you still must work on your deliverance.

The ministry of deliverance is real and is key in the body of Christ. It can be compared to the resurrection of Lazarus. When Jesus called him out of the tomb, he came bound from head to toe. He was resurrected and completely healed—but bound. He couldn't enjoy his freedom until he was unbound.

Sometimes we come to the Lord in that state: saved but bound, unable to enjoy the freedom we have in the Kingdom of God. We see such people in the Church. No matter how hard they try, they're still bound and unable to enjoy the freedom of the Lord.

People suffer all kinds of demonic oppression, bondage, and strongholds. We see Christians who genuinely love the Lord but still struggle with addiction, who despite all their efforts can't shake off the sins that cling to them. They are bound and can't free themselves. They need help.

Jesus's power is available to give you total freedom so you can experience the joy of salvation. Seek Him in prayer, fasting, and intercession. Look for true anointed servants of God for help until the devil's hold on you is broken.

Satan has many tools to keep people under his influence despite the spectacular deliverance Jesus provided. The most efficient one is fear. He will tell you how inadequate you are. "You won't achieve the thing you seek. You'll die along the way. No one will be there to help you. What God is asking is too hard for you. Just give up and die." It's normal to feel a dose of fear, since it helps you strive to be your best. It inspires you to put in all necessary effort to prevent failure. It stops you from being reckless and overconfident. That kind of fear isn't even fear, though; it's caution, born of wisdom.

However, the kind of fear that paralyzes you is sin, because it hinders you from serving God in the capacity He has given you. That's why God counted fear among other despicable sins (Revelation 21:8). Fear, in the form of doubt and discouragement, is unbelief and leads to a mediocre life when God is calling us to excellence.

Anyone can be paralyzed by fear. Elijah was. But we don't have to be paralyzed when the power is available to set us free. We fear many things—dying, going hungry, failing, being defeated, being humiliated, being rejected, etc.—but the good news is that for each kind of fear we also have a scripture that instructs us, "Fear not."

Your key to activating the power of deliverance over fear is the Word. Read and meditate on the Bible daily. God's truth will set you free. Needless to say, it only works when you act on what the Word says (Joshua 1:8). The more time you spend in the Word, the more your faith will grow, and wherever faith is found, fear disappears.

The Son of God was manifested to destroy the work of the enemy (1 John 3:8). Some of Satan's works appear in the form of curses. Curses are real. Though this is not a message on curses, there is one thing I would like to say about them: they set boundaries of what you can do and be.

King Solomon's command to Shimei is the perfect representation of how curses work. The Bible says, *"Then the king sent for Shimei and said to him, 'Build yourself a house in Jerusalem and live there, but do not go anywhere else'"* (1 Kings 2:36, NIV). Curses will tell you, "Yes, you are saved. Yes, you are going to heaven. But here on the earth, this is your boundary. In your family, people don't live beyond forty! In your family, people don't marry; even if they do, they divorce. They don't own anything. They don't reach the breakthrough!"

There is always a limit. It's like a prison in which you are fed, you have a roof, and you are clothed, but you are deprived of your right of freedom to reach beyond the boundary.

Jesus's power is available to break you free from the chains of a curse. It will break down gates of bronze as if they were rotten wood and cut through bars of iron as if they were dry twigs. Like Paul and Silas, activate that power with praise and worship, and the gates of your prison will break open.

Praise and worship, however, is about more than singing and dancing to the Lord. The worship that breaks curses can be seen in a life of total surrender, when you offer yourself as a living sacrifice in submission to His Word and will.

Paul said, *"Therefore, I urge you, brothers and sisters, in view of God's mercy, to offer your bodies as a living sacrifice, holy and pleasing to God—this is your true and proper worship"* (Romans 12:1, NIV). Such worship touches the throne of God, shakes the thresholds, moves the doorposts, and sets the captive free (Isaiah 6:3–4).

Deliverance from Our Enemies

We have one enemy: the devil. The people who hurt us are his servants. They are serving Satan's purpose to steal, kill, and destroy, whether they do it intentionally and willingly or ignorantly.

No matter how good you are to people, not everyone will love you or wish you well. If more than ten percent of the people around you genuinely wish you well, you are a very special species. You know how to invest in others. Remember that among Joseph's ten brothers, only Ruben wanted to save him and send him back to their father in one piece.

Therefore, don't be surprised if people hate you without a reason. The same was true of Jesus. And don't be surprised if they show you their acts of hatred, because in the same way that love leads to action, hate also leads to action. Satan will use such people to hinder your achievement.

As I've said, what the devil wants is to kill and destroy you. If he can't destroy you, he will steal from you. He will inspire others to lay traps for you to fall. They will conspire against you, but the God who delivers us from the devil also delivers us from his agents.

When I think about the traps set by our enemies, I remember Psalm 124:

> …if the Lord had not been on our side when people attacked us, they would have swallowed us alive when their anger flared against us; the flood would have engulfed us, the torrent would have swept over us, the raging waters would have swept us away.
>
> Praise be to the Lord, who has not let us be torn by their teeth. We have escaped like a bird from the fowler's snare; the snare has been broken, and we have escaped. (Psalm 124:2–7, NIV)

How many snares have you escaped? You probably have fallen into some, like Daniel in the pit of lions. But by the grace and power of God, the snare broke and you escaped. Other snares may have been incapacitated before you even knew they were there, leaving your enemies to wonder what happened. They will ask themselves, "How did they escape? How did they not fall into the trap that was set with precision?"

It's because God fights your enemies. He goes before you to deliver you. That is why David said, *"Though an army besiege me, my heart will not fear; though war break out against me, even then I will be confident"* (Psalm 27:3, NIV). The enemy may surround you, but the angels have already been camping around you since long before the enemy arrived (Psalm 34:7).

War is part of a Christian's life. Until the day you breathe your last, you will be fighting. But we have the comfort that Jesus gave us authority over the enemy, and therefore we also have authority over his human agents (Luke 10:19).

It's not enough to know that you are more than a conqueror, though, or that no arm forged against you will prosper. You must do something.

After winning a resounding victory over Syria, a prophet approached the king of Israel and said, *"Strengthen your position and see what must be done, because next spring the king of Aram will attack you again"* (1 Kings 20:22, NIV).

You must develop the mindset of a warrior, ready to face your challenge head-on with courage and determination. The devil is persistent and will attack again and again. Sadly, he is not done fighting you.

However, our war with him is not with blood and flesh. You don't fight with those who plan evil against you by giving them a punch or by hiring worthless bandits to beat them to a pulp. You don't retaliate eye for an eye, tooth for a tooth, gossip for gossip, betrayal for betrayal. Because this is a spiritual battle, you must seek the guidance of the Holy Spirit on how to fight.

Daniel fought on his knees in prayer. Jehoshaphat won over a coalition of three nations through the power of praise. Every battle you fight will be unique and require a unique strategy that only the Holy Spirit can give you.

However, one thing is certain: you need to put on your spiritual armour.

God's Ultimate Deliverance

By a mighty hand and outstretched arm, God delivered Israel from Egypt. And by wonders beyond our understanding, we have been set free from the devil's grip.

However, though defeated, Satan is not yet completely crushed. We are waiting for the day of total deliverance.

Then the end will come, when [Jesus] hands over the kingdom to God the Father after he has destroyed all dominion, authority and power. For he must reign until he has put all his enemies under his feet. The last enemy to be destroyed is death. (1 Corinthians 15:24–26, NIV)

God's power will swallow sin and death, just as Moses's serpent swallowed all the magicians' serpents in Egypt. Those who will be saved will rejoice, saying, *"Where, O death, is your victory? Where, O death, is your sting?"* (1 Corinthians 15:55, NIV)

But even now, as we wait for the final destruction of sin and death, we are walking in victory over death. Jesus's death took away the power that death held over God's children; we are no longer terrorized by it. This is why Paul could say that death was a gain. Like him, we can say, *"If we live, we live for the Lord; and if we die, we die for the Lord. So, whether we live or die, we belong to the Lord"* (Romans 14:8, NIV).

We are not ordinary people, because we have been called by the name of the Lord. We are the spiritual descendants of Abraham. We are called Christians, belonging to Christ. And this is how the Bible talks about us:

And who is like your people Israel [the descendants of Abraham]—the one nation on earth that God went out to redeem as a people for himself, and to make a name for himself, and to perform great and awesome wonders by driving out nations and their gods from before your people, whom you redeemed from Egypt? (2 Samuel 7:23, NIV)

Since we are so highly considered in the Kingdom of God, remember that the prestige of being called a Christian carries a responsibility. Do not make void the power of God that delivered you from sin. Take hold of your total deliverance through the Word, prayer, and praise and worship. Live like a free person. Someone paid the price for it!

MY FATHER IS STILL AT WORK

So he told them, "My Father is working until now,
and I too am working."
(John 5:17, NET)

THESE WORDS, *"MY Father is working until now,"* were spoken by Jesus to the Pharisees after He had healed a man on the Sabbath and the Pharisees and other religious leaders became indignant at Him. Who would blame them? It was the Sabbath, so Jesus, considered a prophet, was supposed to be an example of obedience to the law and not break it.

The Sabbath was important in God's eye. In so many instances, God had rebuked Israel for not honouring it. This was one of the reasons He had rejected them and delivered them to their enemies in the past (Jeremiah 17:21–27). He often made declarations to the people like these:

You have despised my holy things and desecrated my Sabbaths. (Ezekiel 22:8, NIV)

Keep the Sabbath day holy… Then the Lord will be your delight. I will give you great honor and satisfy you with the inheritance I promised to your ancestor Jacob. (Isaiah 58:13–14, NLT)

> Observe the Sabbath day to keep it holy (set apart, dedicated to God), as the Lord your God commanded you. (Deuteronomy 5:12, AMP)

Why then did Jesus perform a miracle on the Sabbath? Scripture records that He did this seven times, all of which were done in the open for the Pharisees to see.

- Jesus healed a lame man (John 5:1–17).

- Jesus drove out an evil spirit from a man who was in the synagogue of Capernaum (Mark 1:21–28).

- Jesus healed Peter's mother-in-law at her home (Mark1:29–31).

- Jesus healed a man with a deformed hand in the synagogue (Mark 3:1–6).

- Jesus healed a blind man He met while walking with His disciples (John 9:1–16).

- Jesus healed a crippled woman in the synagogue (Luke 13:10–17).

- Jesus healed a man with dropsy, which happened in the house of a prominent Pharisee (Luke 14:1–6).

Is there any spiritual significance to the number seven? Maybe, maybe not. What we do know is that seven is God's number, a number of completeness. So did Jesus "completely" break the Sabbath seven times?

Jesus did not break the Sabbath, as His accusers stated, over and over. First, Jesus did nothing these Pharisees, who had appointed themselves guardians of the law, had not themselves done. He refuted their accusations with clear logic: if it was okay for parents to circumcise their sons on the Sabbath, when the prescribed eighth day after birth fell on the Sabbath, then it was also okay for Jesus to heal someone on the Sabbath. If it was accepted that a person could save his donkey that had fallen in a pit on the Sabbath, then it was also okay for the Son of Man to deliver someone under demonic bondage on the Sabbath. If it was okay for someone to put food on their plates and eat on the Sabbath, then Jesus's disciples were also allowed to pick a few heads of grains and eat.

I don't think these religious leaders lacked common sense. The big problem was that they didn't want to believe in Jesus. They were jealous because they knew He was superior. He spoke with an authority they did not have. He performed miracles they could not. He cared for the people, which they did not. In their inferiority complex, they looked for ways to stain His ministry.

Jesus didn't break the Sabbath, because He is the Lord of the Sabbath (Mark 2:28). He didn't come to break the law but to fulfill it; in Him, all the law is accomplished. Simply put, this means that if you are in Jesus, and if you follow Him wholeheartedly, you have fulfilled the law.

He was surprised that the Pharisees, who claimed to know the law, didn't recognize or believe in Him despite the fact that Scripture talked about Him all the way back to the time of Moses. Jesus was the true rest the people needed. And as the Creator of the universe, He had the discretion to set the rules governing the Sabbath.

However, the Pharisees had put in place their own rules regarding the Sabbath, a list of things that were allowed and forbidden, like "Do not pluck heads of grains and eat on the Sabbath." The Bible says that they tied up heavy burdens and laid them on the people's shoulders while they themselves weren't willing to move a finger (Matthew 23:4). That's why Jesus labelled them hypocrites. They were more concerned about honouring their traditions than honouring God.

A Miracle on the Sabbath

By performing miracles on the Sabbath, Jesus's intention was not to provoke the Pharisees, at least not in the negative sense. Rather, He sought to awaken their awareness that God's grace supersedes everything. Seven times Jesus confirmed that God is more concerned by saving His children and doing good than following rules and regulations, since in Jesus all rules and regulations find their fulfillment.

On the day the Pharisees confronted Him about His disciples eating grain, He said, *"If you had known what these words mean, 'I desire mercy, not sacrifice,' you would not have condemned the innocent. For the Son of Man is Lord of the Sabbath"* (Matthew 12:7–8, NIV).

Jesus's desire was not that people become legalistic; His priority was to cover them with mercy so they could find rest in Him. Unfortunately, the priority of the Pharisees was to follow the customs they had built and impose them on everyone.

By healing people on the Sabbath, Jesus was sending a message that God is not limited by tradition. He is not concerned by how things have traditionally been done or the customs of men. No. He is only concerned about meeting his people's needs.

For the Pharisees, the tradition dictated, according to Luke 13:14, *"There are six days for work. So come and be healed on those days…"* (NIV) This was how things had always been done—and to them, how they should remain.

Traditions are not bad. They define people's beliefs and culture. But sometimes they make no sense. Even when they do, they can't limit God's intervention. If Jesus was to have followed every custom of men, He wouldn't have healed the woman with the issue of blood, because she would not have been allowed to touch Him. He wouldn't have accepted the woman who anointed His feet because she was a sinner and thus couldn't come near a prophet. He wouldn't have shared a meal with Zacchaeus. He wouldn't have talked to the

Samaritan woman, because it was unacceptable in Jewish culture for a man and woman to be alone without a chaperone.

Performing miracles on the Sabbath means that God's mercy and grace aren't governed by time and space. While it's true that there is a universal grace available for salvation, there is also a special grace that God provides when He is about to do something in your life. No logic barrier, even the Sabbath, or the fact that one lives in Samaria, meaning far from the Jewish standard of holiness, would stop His special grace.

This brings to mind emergency vehicles like ambulances, police cruisers, fire trucks, and other rescue vehicles; they are given an exception to certain rules of the road. In my language, they are called *unstoppable vehicles*. At a stop sign or red light, they don't stop. Even in traffic jams, they don't wait; they climb onto the shoulder and keep going.

The Pharisees asked the man who was healed, "Why are you carrying your mat?" He replied, "The man who healed me told me I can do it" (John 5:10–11).

The same will be true for you when the unstoppable grace of God reaches you. People will say, "How can you be trusted with such an assignment, or such a ministry, when socially and intellectually you do not fit the acceptable criteria?"

How can you, a demon-possessed woman, be the first to see the risen Jesus? How can you, a thief and a tax collector, be among those who wrote the gospels? How can you, an uneducated fisherman, be the pillar of the Church?

The answer? Because the Master of time and circumstances said so. This is the miracle of the Sabbath; it makes the unfit fit.

You Are Not Forgotten

Though desperate, the man at the pool of Bethesda was not like Lazarus, for whom Jesus was late. It's not like he was sitting in a pile of ashes. The Bible doesn't tell us that he was poor or a beggar. Still, he was invalid who needed a divine intervention.

This man looked and felt like he had been forgotten. Despite coming to the right place every Sabbath for thirty-eight years, he had never received a miracle. I can imagine his life, because we've all been like him at some point. Initially he went to the pool with hope, but as time went by and he saw others get their prayers answered, his hope dwindled and turned into desperation.

It's so hard to wait for such a long time and avoid discouragement. That's why the man was filled with bitterness. When Jesus asked him if he wanted to be healed, he replied with a long list of complaints. It was like he was saying, "I've been faithful and I come here regularly, but I guess it's a waste of time."

People are specialists at making you feel like you've wasted your time with God. They'll say things like, "You've been praying all this time and haven't gotten an answer yet? All your classmates are married with children and you're not? Everyone you started with has been promoted, so why haven't you?"

Perhaps you've been the recipient of such words. If you've been in a similar situation, it's tough not be tempted to ask, "Why not me, God? What do you have against me?" I'm reminded of the song "Pass Me Not, O Gentle Savior," in which we sing, "While on others Thou art calling, do not pass me by."[1] I have no idea what was going through the mind of the writer, Fanny Crosby, but I guess she felt forgotten. Sometimes it feels that way.

But you are not forgotten. You have not wasted your time with God.

On some occasions, the Bible uses the expression "God remembered." He remembered Israel, He remembered Hannah, and He remembered Jonas. It's not that He had forgotten them, although we think that way according to our small understanding. He is

---

1. Fanny Crosby, "Pass Me Not, O Gentle Savior," 1868.

omniscient, so how can He forget? How can He forget you when He has carved your name in the palm of His hand? Whenever He looks at His hands, He remembers you.

It was not by accident that Jesus passed by the pool of Bethesda, because He works by design. That day, He knew very well that the lame man would be there, and that it was his day to be healed.

The same was true on the day Jesus crossed the lake of Gerasenes. He wasn't taking a walk through the countryside; He had a mission for the possessed man He came across, who was to become a missionary.

Be assured of this: whatever desperation you feel, God is your Father and has the best plans for you. You will never be forgotten.

God Still Works

The first recorded miracle Jesus performed was one of transformation, where He transformed water into wine at a wedding (John 2:1–12), but it was probably not the first miracle He performed. Mary's words to the servants that day, as well as her interaction with the Lord, indicate that she was already aware of Jesus's ability to perform miracles, or perhaps she had witnessed Him doing so.

It is no coincidence that transformation is the first miracle we get to witness in Jesus's ministry. The most important miracle that God will accomplish in you, after your salvation, concerns not what He does *for* you but what He does *in* you. Your inner man will inherit the Kingdom, not your finances and not your health.

Therefore, God's preoccupation is to transform you into the image of His beloved Son, turning you into new wine.

It has been said that God doesn't call the qualified; He qualifies the called. We are called in our raw state, and then God starts His work of transformation. He is still at work in you even now, purifying you, correcting you, moulding you, and making you a new creature until He can look at you and see the image of Jesus.

This is like the story of the smith. People asked the smith how and when he could be certain that the gold and silver he worked with had been purified. He answered that he could be assured of this when he was able to look at the metal and see a clear reflection of himself.

Among the apostles, there weren't many who could be considered great—but because they had lived with Jesus, God had worked through them, refining them in such a way that the Pharisees couldn't believe their boldness and knowledge of the Scriptures. That is, until they remembered that they had been with Jesus (Acts 4:13).

The Bible says,

Brothers and sisters, think of what you were when you were called. Not many of you were wise by human standards; not many were influential; not many were of noble birth. But God chose the foolish things of the world to shame the wise; God chose the weak things of the world to shame the strong. God chose the lowly things of this world and the despised things—and the things that are not—to nullify the things that are… (1 Corinthians 1:26–28, NIV)

Peter was impulsive, Nathanael was sceptic, Matthew was a tax collector, Thomas was pessimist, and John and James were envious. The rest of them were no better. However, these are the same people that the Bible tells us turned the world upside-down (Acts 17:6).

Can you imagine a greater miracle than transforming Peter into the pillar of the Church? The guy who trembled in front of a servant girl went on to challenge the religious rulers without any hint of fear. He laid the groundwork for the first church, the one from which we all branched.

You are also a witness of the great work God has done in you, from the day you started your spiritual walk with Him until today. And you aren't yet a finished product, for He is still at work in you.

He works in us through His Word, which is sharper than a double-edged sword. Through it, the believer is built and strengthened, as Timothy says: *"All Scripture is God-breathed and is useful for teaching, rebuking, correcting and training in righteousness, so that the servant of God may be thoroughly equipped for every good work"* (2 Timothy 3:16–17, NIV). Through the Word, the mind is renewed from the carnal state to the mind of Christ.

God also works through suffering to forge our character, without which none are able to stand firm in this corrupt world.

It has been said that charisma will take you to the top but character will keep you at the top. We have all witnessed great people whose charisma took them to the top, but their flawed character couldn't keep them there. The apostle Peter was a man of charisma, but he lacked character. Jesus changed his name from Simon (meaning, a reed) to Peter (meaning, a rock), for he couldn't have been a pillar in the Church with a fickle, reed-like personality.

As Paul said, character is developed through suffering (Romans 5:3). Suffering is the instrument through which God prunes Christians; the bad leaves are removed so the tree can bear fruit. When the tree starts producing fruit, it is pruned even more to help it bear more fruit! This is an unending cycle of pruning.

One interesting aspect of God's transformative work is that it's done in the secret. Only He is aware of what He's doing in you. You don't know what He's doing, nor do the people around us know. We only realize what's happened when we see the final result.

An image comes to my mind when I think of God working in secret. While I was living in Rwanda, the local government paved our neighbourhood with asphalt. When they reached the point where our street branched from the main road, they stopped, leaving a small portion undone.

For several weeks, nothing changed. My friend and I would drive by and curse the contractor and supervisors. We accused the local government of negligence and incompetence.

What we didn't know is that this area was prone to floods, so the engineers had taken the time to dig deep underground and install a solid structure beneath the roadway. When they finished and we realized what had happened, we were so ashamed of ourselves.

That's what we so often do to God. We don't see what He's doing and so we make accusations. How can He leave us in the middle of nowhere, an unfinished product? It's because He is doing underground work, creating in us a solid structure that will withstand the floods of the future.

Jesus Is Working

God is still at work, and Jesus works too. This is the answer He gave to His accusers in Scripture. While He was still here on the earth, He served His Father every day, regardless of the condition—sun or rain, support or no support, Sabbath or any other ordinary day.

In John 9:4, He says, *"I must work the works of Him who sent Me while it is day; the night is coming when no one can work"* (NKJV). This verse implies obligation, a sense of urgency.

For Jesus, doing the work of the Father wasn't something to merely ponder. Even when He faced death on the cross, His only concern was doing His Father's will. He prayed to God, saying, *"My Father, if it is possible, may this cup be taken from me. Yet not as I will, but as you will"* (Matthew 26:39, NIV).

Jesus is still working now. After He accomplished His salvation work, after He said *"It is finished"* on the cross (John 19:30, NIV), He stood at the right hand of the Father to intercede for you and me (Acts 7:55, Romans 8:34). As the Chief Shepherd, He takes care of the needs of His sheep, the Church.

Despite all the powers of hell that wage war against it, the Church still stands powerfully. Neither the devil nor the unfaithfulness of God's servants will affect the power of the Church. Never. As the Groom, Jesus is perfecting the Bride, cleansing her with the washing of water by the Word so that His Church will be made glorious, without spot or a wrinkle, at His coming.

If Jesus is working, the servant should also work. He is our role model. If the master is at work, the servant is expected to do the same, every one according to how he has been called.

It can never be overemphasized that serving God is a must. It's not optional. If God has invested in you, it is logical for Him to demand a return.

In John 4:34, Jesus compared serving the Father to eating food: *"My food is to do the will of Him who sent Me, and to finish His work"* (NKJV). None can survive without food. This is how we must consider serving God; it is our food for life. If God's grace has defied all of your traditions, don't allow the thinking of man to set boundaries around what you can do for and with the Lord.

HE BRINGS LIFE TO THE DESERT

*I will open rivers in desolate heights, and fountains
in the midst of the valleys; I will make the wilderness
a pool of water, and the dry land springs of water. I
will plant in the wilderness the cedar and the acacia
tree, the myrtle and the oil tree; I will set in the
desert the cypress tree and the pine and the box tree
together, that they may see and know, and consider
and understand together, that the hand of the Lord
has done this, and the Holy One of Israel
has created it.*
(Isaiah 41:18–20, NKJV)

WHEN PEOPLE TALK about their wilderness experiences, the first thing that comes to a believer's mind is the forty years Israel spent wandering the desert of Sinai. It was a difficult journey with poor living conditions that caused the people mental distress bordering on insanity. The wilderness is not a place to live for a long time.

Unfortunately for Israel, because of their disobedience, a journey that could have taken them only two years eventually took them forty, until the rebellious generation had died, as God decreed.

Therefore, when Christians talk of the desert, they are referencing a time of struggling to survive and stay afloat. It is a difficult period of harsh conditions that push a person almost to the point of breaking. When hope dwindles, like Israel, such a person may fall in the devil's snare and murmur against God.

In the natural world, there is no life in the desert. One can only survive there for a short period, and no one prospers. However, with God all things are possible. He can make rivers flow in the desert, turning it into a habitable land where a person can prosper as they wait to reach their promised land.

Pressure of Life

The wilderness is a place of harsh weather, extreme heat during the day and extreme cold at night. When you aren't being scorched by the burning sun, you're grinding your teeth and shivering from the cold. The desert presents a succession of hardships and none can feel comfortable in such an environment.

The desert can be used as a metaphor for the pressures of life, which is often full of continuous despair. It is said that someone who's under a lot of pressure is "under heat" or "in hot water." The pressure may be related to their finances, health, work, or family. At some point, we've all experienced high-pressure situations, but there are times when a person is cornered from all sides. When that happens, life can become unbearable. The issues come one after another, without giving you time to breathe.

This is the spiritual wilderness.

David lived for a time in the desert of Zin. During this period, he also crossed his spiritual desert. It had been prophesied that he would become king over God's people, but in this foreign land of uncircumcised Philistines, the highest position he could attain was the king's bodyguard! What greater humiliation could there have been?

On the day when the Philistines decided to attack Israel, he set out with them to attack his country, the land of his father and mother and all his relatives. He didn't do this because he wanted to, because he had turned his back on his country, but because he was in the desert and had to do anything it took to survive.

Finally, when he was rejected by other Philistine princes and returned home, he found his camps destroyed by still other enemies. All his people had been taken hostage and he was almost lynched by his own men. Which way could he turn? He was attacked from all sides. He was a political refugee, He had to lie in order to obtain food and shelter. He was surrounded by enemies and betrayed by those he called friends.

A Place of Deprivation

The wilderness is a place of hunger and thirst. There are no streams or sources of water, and there are no farms. People don't plant crops or rear animals. In the desert, there is only lack. Or rather Lack, with a capital L!

Without water, life becomes almost impossible. Human beings and animals cannot survive long without water. There are times when life feels impossible. You may feel as though you've reached the end of the rope. Your life may seem to be coming to an end. There is no food in the pantry, the bills haven't been paid for months, the bank is calling every day for the mortgage, the car is broken, and the utilities have been cut off. Everything comes to a standstill. Like a giant hand, poverty is choking life out of you.

This is the desert!

The widow of 2 Kings 4 lived a life of lack. Her husband, a prophet, didn't earn enough money to leave an inheritance to his children, so this woman struggled a lot when he died. It was an unliveable situation. She was debt-ridden and her creditors threatened to sell her sons into slavery. To reach that level, I imagine, she had probably sold everything of value—and when she had nothing of value left, she sold even those items of little value, until she had nothing left to give away. I'm certain she could not afford three meals a day, and don't even mention clothing; she was probably covered in rags. This was Lack!

A Polluted Environment

Because of the absence of trees, a small wind can raise a large quantity of dust in the desert. Dust pollutes the clean air we breathe and renders the sky sombre. It's a toxic environment. Such places exist, places that are spiritually or emotionally so polluted that people suffocate there.

Any relationship in our lives can become a wilderness. A small misunderstanding can escalate into fights that could have well been prevented in a heathier relationship. A sane discussion quickly spirals into a heated argument. Neither party has any tolerance or compassion for the other. What kind of life is it when people must walk on tiptoes? Progress is impossible in such an environment.

Abraham and Lot lived in a polluted environment. Their respective servants couldn't stand each other; they were always arguing and fighting. The contention between them grew to the point where Abraham and Lot couldn't live together anymore either. They were forced to separate.

Isaac experienced the same when he lived in the land of the Philistines. He had to move a few times because the locals contended with his servants over his father's wells—that is, until he reached a place where he dug a well and called it Rehoboth, meaning *"For now the Lord has made room for us, and we shall be fruitful in the land"* (NKJV).

A Place of Loneliness

The wilderness is a place of loneliness. You are surrounded by sand in every direction and you can't see far, whether north, south, east, or west. You wander around but get nowhere. Even if you cry for help, who would hear you? You feel abandoned and left to fend for yourself. You have no companion or support, and most of the time you are left to despair.

Challenges and hardships are normal in life, because our world is a world of pain. When you have companions to stand with you, they will encourage you, saying, "Take courage. We are stronger together." Or they may simply offer their shoulders for you to cry on. Their presence makes the pain somehow bearable.

But when you're left by yourself at a time when you need people most, the feeling of betrayal cuts deep.

Paul suffered a lot when he was abandoned in a prison in Rome, facing execution. In his second letter to Timothy, he expressed his pain of being abandoned during his trial. No one had stood with him in defence.

You can feel the sting of betrayal through his writing. It was the cry of a man who had been deeply wounded, especially since Paul was an old man at that time in his life and needed emotional support more than ever (2 Timothy 4:9–16). He was in a place of loneliness in a foreign land, despite all his years of ministry and the many people he had impacted.

What Does the Bible Say about the Wilderness?

Human beings, especially Christians, are quick to judge when they see a person passing through the wilderness. We may call them sinners or judge that they must be living in disobedience. Perhaps God has something against them, to explain why they're going through such a terrible situation.

Job's friends were no different. They visited him when he was passing through his roughest time. They were supposedly there to comfort him, but they spent most of their time accusing him of disobedience to God. Which wasn't true.

People often confuse difficult times with punishment, but this isn't always the case. Israel journeyed in the wilderness for almost two years before they arrived at the plain of Jericho. At that time, God hadn't yet punished them to wander for forty years. The prior two years had been part of God's own design for them.

What had David done that caused him to wander for so long in the desert of Zin, fleeing Saul, starving, and being looked down on by everyone? Nothing. And yet this was a necessary phase of his life.

Those who have been called by God often experience the wilderness in this way. The Bible says that the desert is a place of testing, a crucial phase in the life of a believer.

Even Jesus was tested in the wilderness. Matthew 4:1–2 states, *"Then Jesus was led up by the Spirit into the wilderness to be tempted by the devil. And when He had fasted forty days and forty nights, afterward He was hungry"* (NKJV). He was led there by the Spirit. It was the Father's will for him to go into the desert and be tested. He suffered hunger and thirst, alone, for forty days. He endured much during this time.

In Deuteronomy, God instructed Israel to never forget why they had passed through the wilderness:

And you shall remember that the Lord your God led you all the way these forty years in the wilderness, to humble you and test you, to know what was in your heart, whether you would keep His commandments or not. (Deuteronomy 8:2, NKJV)

God's intention is clear. He uses the wilderness to test our hearts to know what is hidden there (Psalm 139:23–24). That is how He is able to heal our wickedness; when something is revealed, it can't hurt us anymore. (Ephesians 5:13).

The wilderness is also a place where God speaks to our hearts. There is no traffic jam in the wilderness, no noise of the city. It is a place of learning. So when God speaks, we listen. And when He teaches, we learn.

Hosea 2:14 says, *"Therefore I am now going to allure her; I will lead her into the wilderness and speak tenderly to her"* (NIV). In this passage, God talks about Israel and of how its people had been unfaithful and disobedient. Therefore, He decided to take them into the wilderness where He could win them back. What they hadn't been able to hear or understand during their time of plenty, they could hear and understand while in the desert. They could change.

It has been proven that suffering is the best teacher. When you don't allow life's challenges to pin you down, you come out a better person.

The best lesson we learn in the wilderness is trusting in the Lord, because everything else, every success, is built on our relationship with Him. As Deuteronomy 8:3 declares,

> So He humbled you, allowed you to hunger, and fed you with manna which you did not know nor did your fathers know, that He might make you know that man shall not live by bread alone; but man lives by every word that proceeds from the mouth of the Lord. (NKJV)

The Promise of Life in the Wilderness

The wilderness is no place to live. It is meant to be a temporary place one passes through. And finding yourself in the desert isn't necessarily a sign of sin or disobedience. But if you know that you have sinned, then sincerely repent and turn to God for a time of refreshment. He is always waiting with open arms to receive a sinner back and restore them to life.

Otherwise know that your wilderness experience is by God's design. It is likely just a cycle of your life. Remind yourself that Jesus was taken into the desert by the Spirit, and that John the Baptist lived in the desert. What is important is not that you are there. It's not the place that matters but who you're with in that place. Remember that the Hebrews, despite living in oppression under the Egyptians, still multiplied to the point that their oppressors lived in dread of them (Exodus 2:12).

The miracle here is not that God takes you out of the desert, which He will eventually do when its purpose is served. The miracle is that you have a life, an abundant life, even while you're going through your wilderness period. God promised to bring life to the desert, and the first sign of life is that He makes rivers flow, rendering the dry and barren land fruitful. If He can create highways in the sea (Isaiah 43:14–19), why not rivers in the wilderness?

Haven't you seen people who are on the verge of collapse due to debt and poverty, yet they still praise God with sincerity and share the little they have with others? Haven't you seen those who live in a polluted environment yet still behave with dignity in front of their abusers? Aren't there those who are pressured by all kind of problems yet still serve God with integrity? They are peaceful and speak positively. They exhibit calmness in all their actions and are exuberant with the joy of the Lord.

How can that be possible? How can they live in such an unliveable place yet live such special lives? God brought life to their wilderness. Despite the dryness outside, water flows from their bellies (John 7:38). This is the life of David while he struggled in the wilderness. He still cared for the outcasts who fled to him when he was himself a refugee. He sang the most beautiful songs to his Lord because his heart was full of gratitude despite the heat. This is also the life of Paul; despite being abandoned in Rome, he had time to pray for those who had deserted him and write letters of exhortation to the congregations.

How does God do this? Secretly and quietly. Most of the time, we only recognize these miracles after they've already been performed. He told His people, *"You called in trouble, and I delivered you; I answered you in the secret place of thunder"* (Psalm 81:7, NKJV). How secret can thunder be? What God meant is that He answers in secret; we don't know how and when He does a thing, but at last the miracle declares itself through shouts and bangs like thunder, making everyone aware of it!

After Jehoshaphat, king of Judah, and Jehoram, king of Israel, marched for seven days against Moab and came to place with no water, God said to them, *"You shall not see wind, nor shall you see rain; yet that valley shall be filled with water…"* (2 Kings 3:17, NKJV). In other words, there will be no precursor signs, yet the miracle will make the noise of thunder.

In secret, God makes rivers flow within you (John 7:37–38). This is why you are an enigma now. People may not see any sign of it, yet you are a living miracle. They have no clue how you are still standing despite the pressure you face.

As I wrote earlier, in 2017 I was very sick and the doctors weren't able to diagnose my condition. When I went to Nairobi for more advanced tests, the doctor there saw my results and told me that I must have had my condition for many years to have gotten to such a poor state. Normally, people who were sick with my condition would lose a lot of weight, but I didn't look sick. So how was it that I hadn't lost any weight? I understood that God had covered me with His favour to guard me from mockery. That is how He covers His children, sparing them the agony of being the talk of the town.

Abundant Life in the Wilderness

Everyone lives, but not everyone lives an abundant life. The word abundance can be defined this way: "exceedingly, very highly, beyond measure, more, a quantity so abundant as to be considerably more than what one would expect or anticipate."[2]

This kind of life can only be found in Jesus. He said, *"I have come that they may have life, and that they may have it more abundantly"*

———————————

2. "Abundant Life," *Water for the World*. Date of access: June 7, 2023 (https://www.waterfortheworld.org/abundant-life).

(John 10:10, NKJV). This life flows from the inside; it has nothing to do with what happens outside.

Therefore, you can only live abundantly in the desert if you stay connected to Jesus, the true vine. Jesus is the tree planted by streams of water. Its branches never dry but rather laugh at the drought and have the perspective of a better future. Only the branch which is cut from the tree will wither and die.

If you live this way, connected to the true vine, material possessions won't determine the quality of your life. After all, there are rich people who live poorly. An abundant life will not depend on your physical fitness, either, because there are those who are very well in the body but are nonetheless unwell in their hearts.

In Jeremiah 32, the Lord told the prophet to buy land while the city was under siege. The prophecy declared that Israel was going to be deported. So Jeremiah asked the Lord,

> Look, the siege mounds! They have come to the city to take it; and the city has been given into the hand of the Chaldeans who fight against it, because of the sword and famine and pestilence. What You have spoken has happened; there You see it! And You have said to me, O Lord God, "Buy the field for money, and take witnesses"!—yet the city has been given into the hand of the Chaldeans. (Jeremiah 32:24–25, NKJV)

God told him that it was a sign that their time of captivity would one day come to an end. Even though they were going through the desert of their lives, they could still live.

Don't stop dreaming or acting. Take care of your body, look beautiful, and do something, even if it's small. Don't let your heart be troubled, for Jesus's peace will allow you to sleep in the midst of a storm. Don't just survive. Live! Stay positive as you cross the desert, because one day it will come to an end.

Everything you do in the desert will determine your level of breakthrough when you come out. The seed Isaac sowed during the famine made him the richest man in the land.

It's true that the wilderness is a scary place. According to Mark 1:13, Satan is waiting for you in the wilderness; wild beasts are waiting to devour you when you faint from hunger and exhaustion. However, Mark also says that God's angels are there, waiting to serve you. God will never let you face the wilderness alone; He will send his angels to make the journey bearable. Some people you meet on the roadside, like Joseph of Arimathea, will be ready to carry your burden and walk with you. They are God's messengers.

I can't stress enough that you have a part to play in allowing God to make the impossible become possible. Your attitude will determine how long you stay in the wilderness. For Israel, the appointed time was two years, but their attitude of unbelief turned it into forty years.

So stay humble and teachable, and keep trusting God. Pray all kinds of prayers so as not to fall into temptation. If your heart is heavy and you don't feel like praying, tell the Holy Spirit to pray for you. He does it so very well! Never cease singing songs of praise to the Lord, especially when the heat of the desert becomes too great. There is power in praise.

Keep yourself active in service too. Use your gifts and talents to benefit the body of Christ. There is no right time to serve the Lord, for every day is the right time. Even when it is not the time for fig trees to bear fruit, Jesus will still expect to see fruit!

If you're going through the valley of humiliation, if you feel rejected or alone, you must serve the Lord. As Jesus said in Matthew 24:46, *"Blessed is that servant whom his master, when he comes, will find so doing"* (NKJV). Serve the Lord and let people wonder how you're doing it. When they ask, tell them your secret: that your God is Almighty God.

seven

GOD'S PLAN TRANSCENDS EVERYTHING

*But the plans of the Lord stand firm forever, the
purposes of his heart through all generations.*
(Psalm 33:11, NIV)

OUR GOD IS a God of order. This is obvious in the creation process, the redemption process, and everything He does. He works with a plan, seeing the end from the beginning, as the Bible says: *"I make known the end from the beginning, from ancient times, what is still to come. I say, 'My purpose will stand, and I will do all that I please'"* (Isaiah 46:10, NIV).

We are part of His universal plan for all humankind, which is that God *"wants all people to be saved and to come to a knowledge of the truth"* (1 Timothy 2:4, NIV). Though there is a universal plan, God created each and every one of us with and for a purpose. Regardless of the circumstances of our birth, no one came about by accident. There is a plan for you, a place for you, something you alone can accomplish.

What is that plan then? It is His will, His calling, and the mission He has for everyone, including providing everything we need to fulfill that mission.

As believers, we know that we've been created according to a divine purpose for a divine mission; we were created for good works, which God prepared well before we were born (Ephesians 2:10). God had a plan when He created us and it follows us everywhere we go.

He's the mastermind behind our lives, causing everything to fall into place like pieces of a puzzle.

With God, there is no surprise, no accident, and no chance. Everything is planned to the finest detail. You might not know what He has in mind for you, but the one thing you need to know is that you are here by design. Simply put, the blueprint of your life is in God's control. For Jeremiah, God said, *"Before I formed you in the womb I knew you, before you were born I set you apart; I appointed you as a prophet to the nations"* (Jeremiah 1:5, NIV). The same principle applies to everyone who is born of blood and flesh.

What shall we say then? We can boldly declare, like Paul, that everything *"works for the good of those who love [God], who have been called according to his purpose"* (Romans 8:28, NIV). The people you meet, the places you visit, the church you attend, and the person you marry are all details that fall into God's bigger plan for your life. Even when we at times make evil choices, although it may look that we are moving outside of His plan, He can still bring us back the original plan—if we allow Him.

You Still Have the Last Say

God has a plan for your life. However, you still have the choice to either accept or reject it. Since creation, God has given man the power to choose. He told Adam to name the animals, and God respected those chosen names.

He instructed Adam and Eve not to eat of the tree of knowledge of evil and good, telling them that they would die if they did. They did, and they died. He is a true gentleman; He doesn't impose His will. He shows everyone the way, revealing what is good and beneficial, and then lets them decide whether to follow.

Deuteronomy 30:19 says, *"I have set before you life and death, blessing and cursing; therefore choose life, that both you and your descendants may live"* (NKJV). Everything in life is a result of a choice you make; you have the free will to choose what will bring life or what will cause death.

The good news is that no bad choice has to be final. With God, we are assured of second, third, and infinite chances for total restoration if we come back to Him. Even if a person's bad choices land her in a pit, God can still reconnect her to His bigger plan for her life… if she repents.

Solomon was not part of the original plan. If David hadn't sinned by taking someone else's wife, Solomon would not have been born. But God still included him in the plan of salvation.

Our mess isn't wasted when we place it in God's hands. As it has been said, He turns our mess into a message. The mess becomes the compost that nourishes your life for growth.

God Follows His Word

God honours His Word, following it to make sure it is accomplished. No devil or demon can reverse or hinder what God intends to do with your life. As Jeremiah 1:12 says, *"The Lord said to me, 'You have seen correctly, for I am watching to see that my word is fulfilled'"* (NIV).

He followed Jonah in the belly of the great fish. Though Jonah had disobeyed, what God had planned didn't change. Isaiah confirmed, too, that no word proceeding from God's mouth will return void (Isaiah 55:11). What is His Word other than His divine plan and agenda for us? He makes known His ways to man through His Word, so that we should not walk in darkness but be illuminated by His light.

God reveals His purpose for us because He knows that it is our only source of strength in times of trial. There is no accomplishment without a test. The Word of God will test you, over and over (Psalm 105:17–19). Knowing His plans for you, knowing that He is creating a better future for you, will sustain you when the ground shakes.

We saw this in Joseph's life, as well as in David's. Jesus's apostles are also living examples. When these people were tempted to give up under the fire of trials, they remembered where God wanted to take them. They were encouraged to fight one more time, persevering until they reached their destination.

With God, you aren't just wandering around, taking a stroll. There is a target, as with any plan. And just like other plans, God has a timeline in which to accomplish what He has in mind for you, as well as sufficient resources to accomplish it.

The Divine Destination

God has a plan to take you somewhere. You were created to accomplish something that only you can do. This is your promised land to accomplish the will of God. He won't start something with you only to abandon you along the way. He'll make sure to take you all the way to the end—if you stick with him.

Your destination is assured. It will be a good place flowing with milk and honey. The problem is the "in between." What happens along the way? The road you take may be the source of much heartache and headaches.

The Bible states, *"The secret things belong to the Lord our God, but those things which are revealed belong to us and to our children forever, that we may do all the words of this law"* (Deuteronomy 29:29, NKJV). For reasons known only to Him, God has decided not to give us all the details of the journey. After the fall of man, God initiated the salvation plan through the nation of Israel, but neither Abraham nor any of his descendants had a clue how long and tortuous the journey would be.

I like reading and watching Korean historical dramas when I can. Unfortunately, I'm not very patient. I don't like to wait, so I sometimes skip directly to the last pages to read the ending. Or I may search online to see how a series ends. If the ending isn't to my liking, I'll stop—and if I like the ending, I'll carry on.

The truth is that I don't pay much attention to the plots in the middle of a story. Whether I like them or not, they hold little importance.

God's story with you has a good ending. It certainly will be to your liking if you don't lose heart and abandon it partway through. When you become overwhelmed by the many detours and twists in the plot, the thought of your destination should stimulate your resolve to carry on.

God's Provision

Are you worried about how you'll get to the finish line? God has enough resources to pay your fare and living expenses along the way. If you stay in God's will, He will provide for all your needs, at every stage of your journey. He may not give you everything you want, but you can rest assured that your needs will be taken care of.

The congregation of Philippi wasn't rich, but the church still provided for the saints. In his appreciation of their faithfulness, Paul wrote to them: *"And my God shall supply all your need according to His riches in glory by Christ Jesus"* (Philippians 4:19, NKJV). This verse teaches us that as long as we walk in God's purpose, He will always provide.

You may not be rich, but you will have more than enough. As we read in 2 Corinthians 9:8, *"And God is able to make all grace abound toward you, that you, always having all sufficiency in all things, may have an abundance for every good work"* (NKJV). And when the time is right, He will give you riches too—when He judges that you are ready to handle it. Gold and silver are His, and the world and everything in it are His. He will not deprive His children from enjoying such blessings.

God provides in many ways, sometimes in miraculous ways that our minds cannot predict or understand. But His provision goes beyond the material. He also provides all the people you will need to accomplish His purpose.

Moses had a calling, a godly plan for his life. But he couldn't carry it out by himself. When he needed a spokesperson, God provided

Aaron. When Moses needed an advisor, God provided Jethro. When Moses needed a tour guide, God provided Hobab. And on and on it went.

Joseph needed Pharoah to reach the final leg of God's plan for him. David needed Goliath to climb onto the political platform and gain visibility.

God will supply all the people you need when you need them, even enemies in abundance to kick you out of your comfort zone and inspire you to more fervent prayer and study. He will give you a comforter when you need a shoulder to cry on. He will give you comrades who will be with you until the end through all the highs and lows.

God's Timing

God is a master of discretion. When He says, "Follow Me," you must follow. However, He doesn't give you the itinerary. With God, everything happens at the right time, or as we often read in the Bible, "the fullness of time"—not before, not after.

Galatians 4:4 declares, *"But when the fullness of the time had come, God sent forth His Son, born of a woman, born under the law"* (NKJV). We cannot bring forward God's timing through our own efforts, nor can we push it backward. The Pharisees wanted to kill Jesus many times, but no one could lay a hand on Him because His hour had not yet come (John 7:30).

Time has no absolute value anyway. A process will take different amounts of time depending on the conditions. So it shouldn't come as a surprise that God's timing is often undetermined. What takes a month for one person may take years to complete for another. Only God knows all the factors, but it will happen in due time.

In Romans 5:6, Paul wrote, *"For when we were still without strength, in due time Christ died for the ungodly"* (NKJV). In due time, He rescued us from Satan. In due time, He will open the right door and close the wrong ones. In due time, that which God has in mind for us will manifest.

It's hard to wait for the unknown. The Father also knows that it isn't easy, so from time to time, when the wait becomes long and unbearable, He sends encouraging words. Believers are always strengthened by God's Word. It's like refuelling a vehicle so it can keep running.

Though it is very hard, we have to wait for God's timing or else risk falling into Sarah's trap and bring about our own solution outside of God's will. Don't get ahead of God. And don't drag your feet when He says "Go!"

Walk at His pace. When the cloud stops, no matter how you feel, you should stop and wait. When the cloud moves, you must set off without delay, regardless of how incomprehensible or scary the situation looks. Otherwise God will have to force you out, and that is not a pleasant experience.

The Plan of God in Action

In early 2000, a devout widow lived with her two daughters in a refugee camp in Rwanda. Her life consisted of prayer, church, and evangelizing. But one day God told her that He would move them to Europe so she could serve Him there as an intercessor for the nations.

I can imagine what went through her mind. Perhaps, like Sarah, she laughed! "God, I don't speak French or English. No one knows me. And how will I get there?"

However, it is amazing to watch how God works.

Here is what happened. This woman's eldest daughter fell sick and the local hospital was unable to treat her, so they transferred her to Kigali, the capital city of Rwanda. When they arrived in Kigali, the doctors decided to transfer the sick child to Nairobi, Kenya. The woman was to accompany her, but she refused to leave her other, younger daughter by herself.

The office of the United Nations High Commissioner for Refugees, which was sponsoring the treatment, agreed to pay for the mother and younger daughter to also travel to Nairobi.

Once in Kenya, the medical team resolved to send her to an even more specialized doctor, this time in Norway. In less than two weeks, the family had a sponsor and their immigration papers were finalized. The rest, as they say, is history.

This is a real-life example showing that the counsel of the Lord stands forever. Some of the things that happen in our lives seem painful and illogical, and we think we could gladly do without them. But they are often God's doing and will lead to His ultimate objective.

Remember that for Saul to be anointed king, God caused his father's donkeys to be lost so he could meet Samuel!

The road may be tortuous, steep, or slippery—and, yes, it may even run through a refugee camp or a hospital. But God will follow His Word to make it happen.

Joseph was seventeen when he received a revelation of God's plan (Genesis 37:2). He knew then that he was destined for greatness. He was thirty when he presented himself before Pharaoh and became the prime minister of Egypt (Genesis 41:46). The journey saw him variously in a pit, serving as a houseworker for Potiphar, and languishing in prison. Along the way he was hated by his brothers, betrayed by his master, and unjustly incarcerated.

These were certainly extraordinary experiences, but take note of where they led.

Pray for the Plan of God.

Jeremiah 29:11 says, *"For I know the plans I have for you… plans to prosper you and not to harm you, plans to give you hope and a future"* (NIV). This was part of a prophecy of Israel's restoration after seventy years of exile.

When those seventy years were complete, Daniel prayed to remind God of His promise. The Bible says,

> In the first year of Darius son of Xerxes (a Mede by descent), who was made ruler over the Babylonian kingdom—in the first year of his reign, I, Daniel, understood from the Scriptures, according to the word of the Lord given to Jeremiah the prophet, that the desolation of Jerusalem would last seventy years. So I turned to the Lord God and pleaded with him in prayer and petition, in fasting, and in sackcloth and ashes. (Daniel 9:1–3, NIV)

According to God's agenda, Israel was to be released from captivity after a set period. So why did Daniel have to pray, since God had already decided to do it?

In our human understanding, it doesn't make sense. Since God can't lie, and He follows His Word to make it happen, why do people have to pray? Why did Jesus pray before He chose the twelve apostles, even though He knew the complete story from the beginning to the end?

There is a divine mystery relating to prayer, a power beyond our understanding that makes things happen. No wonder Jesus told His disciples that they should pray, never giving up, until God answered. He tells us not to be silent and not to give Him rest (Isaiah 62:6–7). If He delays, wait for Him in prayer and service, like the disciples did as they waited for the day of Pentecost.

His delay is the time He gives you to improve your skills. The years David spent wandering, leading a band of outcasts, prepared him to be a good leader for God's people.

You must pray for the promise, even if God has already promised to do a thing. If you don't pray, the devil will put in motion his own plan instead of God's divine one—and the devil's plan is always to steal, kill, and destroy. Whatever God says, Satan will try to counter it; he works the same way as he did in the garden of Eden.

Prayer will also allow you to be sensitive to the voice of the Holy Spirit, with whom you won't walk as a blind person but rather as a person illuminated by the Word. As you walk, you will see doors being closed, even ones which you thought were right for you. Other doors, ones you didn't anticipate, will open.

God's ultimate priority for you might not include that which seems good and logical. Acts 16 is full of accounts of the many missionary trips Paul and his companions planned to take, but they were stopped by the Spirit of the Lord. Though Paul's calling was to evangelize the Gentiles, at that specific time and place it was not part of God's plan. You can only follow Him if you are spiritually connected to heaven. That is how you will walk in God's plan.

HOW WILL THIS BE POSSIBLE?

Then Mary said to the angel, "How can this be,
since I do not know a man?"
And the angel answered and said to her, "The Holy
Spirit will come upon you, and the power of the
Highest will overshadow you; therefore, also,
that Holy One who is to be born
will be called the Son of God."
(Luke 1:34–35, NKJV)

HAS GOD EVER told you something so big that you couldn't wrap your mind around it? Perhaps you were even afraid of sharing it with a single soul because you wondered whether it was just your imagination playing tricks on you. Perhaps you asked yourself, "How is this possible?"

You aren't alone. Many have been in your situation, where the things God wants to do for and through them are so big that they're hard to accept.

Mary the mother of Jesus, who spoke the above words, also found herself in such a situation. In Luke 1:26–37, we find the story of a virgin girl who received a revelation: she would conceive and give birth to a son who would be great and called the Son of the Most High. She had never heard of such a thing. According to her human understanding, she could only ask, "How is this possible?" It was too much for her.

First, she was a virgin. How could she be with a child when she had never known a man? Second, she was poor and came from a small village. Her husband-to-be was also poor. They weren't known to anybody.

How was it that among all the girls, including all those who must be more qualified, she had been chosen to bear the Son of the Most High?

The Bible tells us that in many cases *"God has chosen the weak things of the world to put to shame the things which are mighty"* (1 Corinthians 1:27, NKJV). Still, even knowing this isn't enough for the human mind, which is used to working with logic.

Mary may have asked herself a series of questions, including: how would it happen? A woman couldn't bear a child without a man, but God created the universe from nothing. He *"calls those things which do not exist as though they did"* (Romans 4:17, NKJV).

How would this be possible? It would be a miracle of creation. God is able to start from nil and create anything by the power of His Word alone.

But for such a miracle, He needed a woman with Mary's attitude—an attitude that would allow Him to operate.

The Attitude that Makes Miracles Happen

Mary's attitude was to say, "Yes, I have questions. But I trust You. Since You said it, You will accomplish it. I don't need to be concerned about how You'll do it." Mary didn't waste her time pondering the cost of her calling—and yes, there would be a cost. She was an unmarried woman who would give birth. What would happen to her reputation? Who would ever want to marry a girl with a child? How was she going to support herself and her child given that she was already poor?

These were legitimate concerns, but Mary decided to leave everything in the Lord's mighty hands. She said, *"I am the Lord's servant… May your word to me be fulfilled"* (Luke 1:38, NIV).

Mary's attitude denoted trust, confidence, and faith. It allowed God to work because incredulity stops His intervention. God hates incredulity. He expects that His children will trust Him and believe that He can do what He says He will do. He does not utter words carelessly or jokingly. He is not man. He means what He says and says what He means.

Unbelief is the attitude of the ten spies, not to mention most of the Israelites at that time. It hinders God from making a miracle possible. Recall that those Israelites had experienced God's wonders firsthand as they moved from Egypt into the wilderness. They watched God hit Egypt with ten plagues. They witnessed the Red Sea split in two, allowing them to cross on dry land. They ate the food from heaven and drank water from a rock.

And despite all these miracles, they still didn't believe that God was able to drive the Canaanites out of the land which He had promised for them (Numbers 13:26–33).

That attitude angered God, who swore to Himself:

"As I live," says the Lord, "just as you have spoken in My hearing, so I will do to you: the carcasses of you who have complained against Me shall fall in this wilderness, all of you who were numbered, according to your entire number, from twenty years old and above." (Numbers 14:28–29, NKJV)

The Bible also warns us:

Therefore, since the promise of entering his rest still stands, let us be careful that none of you be found to have fallen short of it. For we also have had the good news proclaimed to us, just as they did; but the message they heard was of no value to them, because they did not share the faith of those who obeyed. (Hebrews 4:1–2, NIV)

An entire generation perished in the wilderness. Only Joshua and Caleb, who received the Lord's message with faith, received what had been promised: a land flowing with honey and milk.

Let us learn from Rahab the prostitute. She had never witnessed a miracle from God and she wasn't of the chosen people, but she had heard of the God of Israel and believed. Her trust, confidence, and faith in our Lord allowed her to lay claim to that which originally had not been hers!

God honours faith. He rewards the trust we put in Him. And that is what makes miracles possible.

The Recipient of the Greatest Miracle

Through Mary, Christmas, the most celebrated day around the world, was made possible. Whether or not people know God, whether they believe in Jesus Christ, people around the world see Christmas as a day to either cash in or enjoy a traditional family get-together.

As Christians, though, it is a day on which we remember the enormous sacrifice that was required for us to be reconciled with God and lay claim to eternal life. We remember God giving His only begotten Son. We remember Jesus sacrificing His position of equality with God and becoming human. We remember Mary giving her life and reputation to be used by God. And through that sacrifice, God gained sons and daughters, Jesus gained brothers and sisters, and Mary became the most blessed human being who will ever live.

This virgin birth of Jesus—together with his death and resurrection, because they must be taken together as a whole—is the most significant miracle ever performed in the universe. It is greater than the act of creation itself, because it resulted in man's redemption and the restoration of the power, authority, and dominion the devil stole from humanity.

Before Jesus, God manifested Himself occasionally through prophets and seers. He fellowshipped with His children through the service of priests. Since the coming of Jesus on the earth, God's power has exploded in its manifestation. The heavens opened and God truly descended to live with His people.

Everyone now enjoys free access to God. Everyone who's willing to be His servant can receive His power.

Something Big in Store for You

Let us return to Mary's question: "How is this possible?" The story of Mary is about her receiving the greatest of all miracles. It's also the story of ordinary people accomplishing extraordinary things with God. As Jesus has assured us, everything is possible to those who believe.

Indeed, this is a story of our life-changing destiny being made possible through the power and authority of Jesus, evidenced in His life, death, and resurrection. Through that transforming power, as believers we can dream and be and do anything that God designed us to be and do, regardless of human limitations.

Not everyone will have a visitation and elevation like Mary, but God has something big in store for everyone who believes. We are God's workmanship, created for good works (Ephesians 2:10). Good work awaits us if we are willing to say, like Mary, "Since You said it, You will also do it." Why? Because, as we read in Luke 1:37, *"no word from God will ever fail"* (NIV).

You may say, "What about me? There has been no special prophecy about me." Well, you don't need a special prophecy. The Bible is your ultimate prophecy. Everything in it is yours to claim. And if you aren't sure, do like Habakkuk; keep guard at your post, on the watchtower, and pray fervently. Don't move until God has said something or given you a word of prophecy. Then wait for its accomplishment without losing heart if it is delayed in coming true, for surely it will take place (Habakkuk 2:1–3).

Jesus's birth was the fulfillment of a prophecy first spoken in Eden when God told the serpent that the woman's offspring would crush its head (Genesis 3:15). Everything God does starts with His spoken Word. His Word activates His power and puts in motion the accomplishment of what He has designed.

In the beginning, the world was without form. Even though the Spirit of God hovered over the void, nothing fell into place until God spoke. That's when the world as we know it today came into existence (Genesis 1:1–3).

There is a word for you, and it speaks of the great things He plans to do with you and through you. Don't give God rest until you have that word. And then don't give Him rest until the word come to pass.

The Test of Time

Mary didn't just appear on the scene out of nowhere. She came about after a long period of preparation that took four thousand years, going back to the founding of a nation through Abraham and the selection of a tribe through Judah.

If there is something you should know about God, it's that He is never in a hurry. He takes time to prepare.

Everyone God has called has been prepared through testing and trial. Abraham was prepared. David was prepared as well. There are no exceptions. The reason for this is that God calls us in our raw state, after which the test of time refines us, teaching us obedience through suffering and allowing us to transform into usable instruments of His glory (2 Timothy 2:21). It is a period of waiting and wandering through the wilderness.

> Remember how the Lord your God led you through the wilderness for these forty years, humbling you and testing you to prove your character, and to find out whether or not you would obey his commands. (Deuteronomy 8:2, NLT)

I hate waiting. No one likes it. Patience is not embedded in our human nature.

Unfortunately, God doesn't give us an alternative. We know this, however: even if the manifestation of God's promise is delayed, it will surely take place.

Joseph endured that test. The Bible says that *"until what he had said came to pass, the word of the Lord tested him"* (Psalm 105:19, ESV). I sometimes try to imagine what went through Joseph's mind when he received the vision of himself as a leader of his brethren. He must have asked, "How will this be possible? I'm the second youngest in my father's family, at the very back of the chain!" Perhaps he also asked God why nothing good seemed to happen to him even after many years of waiting.

And I can also imagine God's answer: *"I, the Lord, will hasten it in its time"* (Isaiah 60:22, NKJV).

Joseph first had to be baked in the furnace of time, test, and trial. When the time was right, God hastened everything according to His Word. Joseph was then rushed out of prison, presented before Pharoah, and became prime minister in the blink of an eye.

It is true that waiting for the right time can be difficult, but waiting isn't bad. This period of time heals our wounds, justifies us, and proves God to be faithful. Most importantly, it gives us the opportunity to grow to maturity so we can handle the weight of God's mission for us.

The Days of Small Beginnings

Isaiah 60 is about the restoration of God's people. It is a promise to the Church of the future.

The words of this prophecy probably seemed too good to be true at the time. After all, Israel had suffered under the feet of its enemies. Therefore, God gives them reassurance: *"A little one shall become as thousand, and a small one a strong nation. I, the Lord, will hasten it in its time"* (Isaiah 60:22, NKJV).

Here we see God's modus operandi. He doesn't start from the top, but rather from the bottom. At first nothing is visible. You may think you've gotten everything wrong, that God hasn't said anything. Then there is a small cloud, like the one Elijah saw, so small that in the big sky it appears to be no larger than a man's hand. But that small cloud grows and gives forth rain that makes you forget all the years of drought and famine.

The start of a journey towards accomplishing your great calling will always look small and negligible, like that cloud. However, God says, *"Do not despise these small beginnings, for the Lord rejoices to see the work begin, to see the plumb line in Zerubbabel's hand"* (Zechariah 4:10, NLT).

However small your beginning looks, give it all you have; he who can't be faithful in the small things can't be faithful in the big things. Don't be concerned about how far others have reached or how successful they look. They too started at the first step of the ladder and climbed high.

Jesus's life serves as an example. Mary received the word that she would give birth to the Messiah, the One who would save the world. But when Jesus was born, He looked like any other baby, weak and unimpressive.

Don't lose heart if you're still preaching to empty chairs. Your time will come. Even the Israelites didn't possess Canaan in one day; little by little they conquered and occupied the land.

Crucified with Jesus

In 1975, Loren Cunningham (Youth with a Mission) and Bill Bright (Campus Crusade for Christ) received a revelation from God that they needed to invade the "seven spheres" of society, also called the "seven mountains of influence," in order to bring godly change to the nations.

According to this revelation, whatever you have been called to do, you will serve the Lord in one of the seven spheres: religion, family, education, government, business, arts and entertainment, and media. How much spiritual influence you have will be determined by how far you want to climb. There are those who will stay at the foot of the mountain, those who will settle in the middle, and those who will climb all the way to the top.

Everyone has a mountain of influence, but not everyone will ascend to the top. There is a price to pay to stand atop your mountain. The Bible asks, *"Who may ascend the mountain of the Lord? Who may stand in his holy place?"* (Psalm 24:3, NIV) The same passage of Scripture gives us the answer: *"The one who has clean hands and a pure heart, who does not trust in an idol or swear by a false god. They will receive blessing from the Lord and vindication from God their Savior"* (Psalm 24:4–5, NIV).

In Paul's words, those conditions may be translated this way: *"I have been crucified with Christ and I no longer live, but Christ lives in me. The life I now live in the body, I live by faith in the Son of God, who loved me and gave himself for me"* (Galatians 2:20, NIV).

Until you reach the state where you live only for Jesus, you won't grasp the full power of God's calling for you. Mary's mission was to give birth to the Saviour of the world. Jesus's death and resurrection is what made that possible. Your death and resurrection in Him is what will make it possible for you to stand atop the mountain God has designed for you.

How Does It Become Possible?

So how does this become possible? The answer is simple: by the power of the Spirit of God. Zechariah 4:6–7 says, *"This is the word of the Lord to Zerubbabel: 'Not by might nor by power, but by My Spirit,' says the Lord of hosts. 'Who are you, O great mountain? Before Zerubbabel you shall become a plain!'"* (NKJV)

This is how Joseph became the prime minister of a foreign country. By the power of the Spirit, he interpreted Pharoah's dream, and no one else in Egypt could be found to rival his wisdom. Was it any one person who opened Joseph's door? No. The Holy Spirit did all the work.

This is also how Daniel became the third most powerful person in Babylon, despite being nothing but an exiled eunuch. It's how Mary became pregnant when she had never been with a man; she gave birth to the Saviour and became the most blessed woman.

It's how God will elevate you to places He has promised to take you. You don't need anyone to give you a push. You don't need a recommendation. God will recommend you and will create the opportunity. He will open the way.

Remember, it will depend on your attitude. If you clench your fist in unbelief, nothing will happen even if God Himself were to come down. It depends on your faith, for the Bible says that a man without faith should not expect to receive anything from the Lord (James 1:6–8).

Despite having witnessed God's power several times, the word of promise Israel received had no value to the people because they didn't receive it with faith (Hebrews 4:1–2).

Because of doubt, Zechariah was made mute. He thought that the word he received from the angel was impossible. But God's promises *should* look impossible, otherwise no one would give their manifestation any consideration. There is a reason for this. Once He has elevated you to the top of the mountain, you should never be able to say, "My hand did it." When His destiny for you is accomplished, rather, everyone will say, "Only God could do this. Only He could make this possible."

nine

THE MIRACLE OF RESURRECTION

*When Jesus came into the ruler's house, and saw the
flute players and the noisy crowd wailing, He said
to them, "Make room, for the girl is not dead, but
sleeping." And they ridiculed Him. But when the
crowd was put outside, He went in and took her by
the hand, and the girl arose.*
(Matthew 9:23–25, NKJV)

THIS PASSAGE PRESENTS a miraculous story of resurrection. It starts in
Matthew 9:18 when the ruler of a synagogue, Jairus, came to Jesus
and entreated him, saying, *"My daughter has just died, but come and
lay Your hand on her and she will live"* (NKJV). Jesus followed this
father right away.

However, in Mark and Luke, the Bible states that the girl was not
dead yet. Rather, she was at the point of death.

While Jesus was on His way to heal the girl, Jairus received
messengers from his house with bad news, saying, *"Your daughter is
dead. Do not trouble the Teacher"* (Luke 8:49, NKJV). In other words,
"Let Him be. He can't do anything now. It's no longer possible. It's
too late."

They said this because they didn't know that Jesus, the Master
and Teacher, could raise the dead. But He *can* raise the dead! Our
God has the power to raise the dead, not only those who have just
died but also those whose bodies have started to decompose, as in

the case of Lazarus—or even those who died long ago, like the dried bones in Ezekiel.

The Life-Changing Miracle of Resurrection

Jesus performed all kinds of miracles, but in my opinion the greatest of all was when He raised the dead. On this side of life, after all, death is the end of everything if we don't take eternity into consideration.

We read in Ecclesiastes 9:5, *"For the living know that they will die, but the dead know nothing; they have no further reward, and even their name is forgotten"* (Ecclesiastes 9:5, NIV). The writer further advises, *"Whatever your hand finds to do, do it with all your might, for in the realm of the dead, where you are going, there is neither working nor planning nor knowledge nor wisdom"* (Ecclesiastes 9:10, NIV).

For other conditions, even if they are bad, one can still say that there is hope. But after death, all hope is gone. Therefore, Jesus's acts of raising the dead show us that nothing, absolutely nothing, is impossible for God.

The story of raising Jairus's daughter is unique in one important respect. When He raised Lazarus and the son of Nain's widow, it was done publicly. In the presence of all the people, Jesus called to life the dead, and the dead came to life. But with Jairus's daughter, Jesus requested that the crowd go outside. We don't know why, but God never does anything just for the sake of doing it.

One reason could be that Jesus wanted to teach us an important lesson, that there are miracles we only obtain away from the eyes of spectators. Sometimes God will ask you to climb the mountain alone. The Bible says that God called Moses to the top of Mount Sinai and he went up. That's where he met God, heard His voice, and received His instructions, alone with God, without any interference of the crowd below.

God can do anything, anywhere, and at any moment. But there are days when you need to get far away from the crowd, away from distractions, in order to receive what He plans for you.

There is a mountain in Rwanda renowned as a place where people can have their prayers answered. One day, my sisters invited me to go there with them. This occurred during a period when I desperately needed a miracle to send my children back to school. They were studying at the time in a private school in the United States, but our financial situation had made it impossible to pay the tuition any longer.

I honestly don't believe that you need to travel to a specific place to get your prayer answered. But I remembered that Jesus would go up the mountain to be alone with the Father, and that the apostles would go into the wilderness to pray. This convinced me to go with my sisters.

The mountain was very steep and ascending its slope was most difficult. After two hours of climbing without reaching the top, I gave up and sat down. Like a child, I cried. "I will not move from here, no matter what," I told my sisters.

Alas, I had no choice but to keep going. Descending from that point would have been even harder, due to the steep incline and rocky terrain. It would have taken more than three hours, and I knew there was a much easier descent on the other side.

Finally, with difficulty, I reached the top. While there I came to truly understand what it means to seek God with all our hearts (Jeremiah 29:13).

To cut the story short, I received my miracle and my children went back to school. I'm not sure if it happened because I climbed the mountain, but I am sure of one thing: I was in a situation where I couldn't afford to be complacent. I needed to get away from the crowd and, like Jacob, wrestle with the angels while others slept.

Let's turn our attention once again to the widow who came to see Elisha in 2 Kings 4. This woman had nothing that would help to prevent her children from being sold into slavery. I imagine that she had exhausted all other options. Maybe she had tried to borrow money from friends and family, to no avail. Perhaps by this point in time nothing else seemed possible. Her situation was dead and she needed a resurrection in order to pay her debts and survive.

Elisha told her,

Elisha said, "Go around and ask all your neighbors for empty jars. Don't ask for just a few. Then go inside and shut the door behind you and your sons. Pour oil into all the jars, and as each is filled, put it to one side... Go, sell the oil and pay your debts. You and your sons can live on what is left." (2 Kings 4:3–4, 7, NIV)

Sometimes you'll need to close the door and seek God in private before you can come out a changed person, especially when you're dealing with a desperate situation in which you know you're dead unless God intervenes.

Learn How to Manage the Crowd

The crowd is part of life and we need to know how to live within one such that it doesn't affect our lives, like the rabble in Exodus affected the children of Israel. If you're looking for a life-transforming experience, you will have to learn how to keep the crowd at arm's length.

Who is the crowd anyway? They are those people around you who have no stake in what you're doing or your relationship with God. They aren't necessarily bad people, and they may not stand against you, but they aren't very helpful either. Crowds are good in terms of cheering you on when things are going well, but in the end you still have to stand by yourself.

Look at it from the eye of a soccer player. The cheering crowd gives him a sense of support and worth, but he is ultimately alone on the pitch with his teammates. Even though he feels supported, the crowd does little to help him score goals.

Don't get me wrong: we need the crowd! Can you imagine the soccer pitch without the brouhaha of fans? It's part of the fun of the game. We are social beings and need social interaction. However, in terms of achievement, they can't help us because they aren't equipped for that. Why not?

First, the crowd is noisy. It always makes a commotion, making it difficult for those around us to hear. Everyone has their own opinion and talks at the same time, making it difficult to convey useful advice. What help can they give anyway since they don't have the necessary wisdom? It's not that they lack wisdom individually, but because they have little to no stake in your business they know nothing of what's really happening in your life.

Jesus knew that teaching the crowd wouldn't yield much in terms of results, which is why He chose a small group, an inner circle of disciples, to impart all His teaching and anointing—and they, in turn, could reach others.

As for the multitude, the Bible says that Jesus spoke to them in parables. When His disciples asked why He spoke in parables,

He answered and said to them, "Because it has been given to you to know the mysteries of the kingdom of heaven, but to them it has not been given. For whoever has, to him more will be given, and he will have abundance; but whoever does not have, even what he has will be taken away from him. Therefore I speak to them in parables, because seeing they do not see, and hearing they do not hear, nor do they understand." (Matthew 13:11–13, NKJV)

The crowd pressured Jesus, but they didn't touch him. In Luke 8:45–46, the Bible says,

> And Jesus said, "Who touched Me?"
>
> When all denied it, Peter and those with him said, "Master, the multitudes throng and press You, and You say, 'Who touched Me?' "
>
> But Jesus said, "Somebody touched Me, for I perceived power going out from Me." (NKJV)

Among the multitude that followed Jesus, few experienced His power. Only Jesus knew who among the crowd thronged and pressed Him and who touched Him, because He could see the heart whereas we only see the exterior.

The same is true of crowds today.

Still, He told us that we will know people by their fruit (Matthew 7:16). The crowd, at heart, bears no fruit. These are the people who have been in church for years, who even serve in ministries, but have never touched Jesus. In other words, they have never been deeply impacted by their relationship with God. They are still the same carnal Christians as they were on the day they started following Him.

The crowd is led by emotions and rarely by reasoning, thus they are fickle and unreliable.

In his gospel, John offers proof of the crowd's unpredictability. Those who followed Jesus *"intended to come and make him king by force"* (John 6:15, NIV). But Jesus knew that these people didn't follow Him because they believed in Him but because He had filled their bellies with bread (John 6:26–27). They were moved by the excitement of the moment and shallow gratitude.

After all, these were the same people who wanted Him dead just a few months later. On Palm Sunday, as Jesus entered Jerusalem on a colt, the crowd threw their cloaks down and danced with shouts of joy. Four days later, they cried out for Him to be crucified. When Pilate asked them to choose who should be spared crucifixion between Jesus and Barabbas, who was a criminal,

> They shouted back, "No, not him! Give us Barabbas!" Now Barabbas had taken part in an uprising. (John 18:40, NIV)

Can you believe such people? They had been with Jesus for three years. He had healed their sick, delivered their possessed, and filled their hungry stomachs. But as soon as the priests asked for His death, they blindly followed without giving it a second thought.

The crowd isn't loyal. When they get their way, they'll be your best friends. Otherwise they'll be the first to turn their backs and talk of stoning you.

The crowd doesn't understand your ambitions and will try to shut you up.

Bartimaeus was blind. His only dream was to see. Therefore, when by divine grace an opportunity came for him to receive a miraculous healing, he didn't wait; he shouted to Jesus, pleading for a miracle. The crowd who heard him, who knew how important it was to see and knew how pitiful he was, instead of encouraging him, rebuked him and told him to be quiet (Mark 10:46–52).

This is typical of the crowd; you can't expect much support from them. They'll kill your dreams. They'll say, "Why do you even want to be healed? Why do you want to see? Aren't you satisfied the way you are today?" They'll tell you to stop that nonsense: "You can't do it. You aren't equipped. You don't have enough money. You don't have the required education!"

This reminds me of Joseph's brothers, who literally said to him, "Stop dreaming." Despite being close relatives, they were the crowd. They had no stake in God's calling upon Joseph and never tried to understand his dream or help him achieve it. Instead they acted with jealousy.

Break Away from the Crowd's Influence

Remember, the people in the crowd aren't necessarily bad people who are looking to harm you. But if you allow them to control you, they'll kill your faith and instill confusion instead of confidence.

If you want to receive God's power, you must break away from their influence so you can clear the communication channel with God and hear His voice. You must learn to be that person who touches Jesus when others are pressing Him, like the woman in Mark 5.

This woman had to overcome a major obstacle. She had an issue of blood, meaning that she wasn't allowed to be in the assembly; everything she touched became unclean. She couldn't touch anyone, much less the Son of God.

But she didn't focus on the obstacle. Instead she focused on her desperation, her pain. She had lost everything in her quest for help. For twelve years, she had visited every physician she could find. Jesus was her last option, and she went for it regardless of what stood in her way: the people who strongly believed in their tradition.

If you focus on the challenges in front of you, if you worry about what people will say, then you aren't desperate enough. Your pain isn't unbearable enough. Your desire to achieve your dream isn't strong enough—yet. With a limited attitude, you can't touch Jesus. You're still following the opinion of the crowd.

Don't forget that each one of them has their own opinions. One will say "Go right" while the other says "Go left." Which one will you follow?

In the pursuit of your goal, give it everything you've got. Only then will you be able to push the crowd aside and touch Jesus. If you're only half resolute, you'll only reach the halfway point. Once you're done with earthly solutions, you'll get the heavenly answer.

What about the woman from Mark 5? The Bible tells us, *"When she heard about Jesus, she came behind Him in the crowd and touched His garment. For she said, "'If only I may touch His clothes, I shall be made well'"* (Mark 5:27–28, NKJV).

It must not have been easy for her to reach Jesus. There would already have been a large gathering. She had to approach from the rear, pushing people right and left to make way for herself, since no one would do it for her. She could only count on herself.

At the end, she received what she had gone out for. The Bible gives us Jesus's answer to her courage and faith: *"And He said to her, 'Daughter, your faith has made you well. Go in peace, and be healed of your affliction'"* (Mark 5:34, NKJV). Not only did she achieve her desire, but she was recognized by Jesus. He called her His daughter! Throughout the four gospels, she is the only person who Jesus refers to in this way.

Don't confuse pushing people aside with being heartless, egotistical, or uncaring of others in the pursuit of your goal. It doesn't mean that you'd do whatever you want regardless of who you trample in the process. That's akin to being a brute, and rarely do such people attain anything sustainable. They climb on others' backs but don't get anywhere.

Rather, pushing people aside in this way declares that you won't allow what people do, say, or think, whether good or bad, to dictate the course of your action. Regardless of their support, you go forward.

When I think about this daughter of Christ in Mark 5, I can't help but think about athletes competing in a race. They start in a crowd and run for a certain distance. As they draw closer to the finish line, some start to run faster, leaving the crowd behind. They're using the last ounce of their strength and will to win. No one among them feels sorry that they're leaving their colleagues in the dust.

This is the spirit that should drive everyone who seeks to touch Jesus and claim a miracle.

Learn from Jesus

Jesus is our role model. Anything we want to do right, let us look up to Him. I'm sure you would tell me that Jesus could do everything right because He was the Son of God. Yes, He was God. But the Bible says that He was also totally human, subject to the same challenges as we are subjected to.

The Spirit testifies that He came in the flesh (1 John 4:2–3) and was completely man. The Bible adds that Jesus, as a man, was tempted as all men are (Hebrews 4:15), though He didn't sin. He was given a free will, but He chose to submit to God (Luke 22:42, John 10:18). Since He was human, we can be sure that His example is humanly possible.

Jesus had a following of more than ten thousand people. You may wonder how I came up with this number. When Jesus fed the multitude in the first miracle of multiplication, the Bible says, *"The number of those who ate was about five thousand men, besides women and children"* (Matthew 14:21, NIV). Even today, more women follow Jesus than men, so the number of women and children surely exceeded the five thousand men.

In today's term, it's like having many megachurches of people listening to your preaching every Sunday, eagerly reading your books, and attending your crusades. However, you can't build your life on these people; their presence, or absence, shouldn't influence how you serve God—or how you strive to live a better life, succeed, and prosper.

Learn from Jesus. He never sought the approval of the crowd, only of the Father. He never tried to explain Himself or please them. He didn't rely on their support and understanding to advance; He relied only on the power of heaven and the Word of His Father.

He was never drunk on their praise, like the day they planned to make Him king. Instead of listening to their flattery, He withdrew to the mountain by Himself (John 6:15), because He wanted to be in the presence of the Father and draw from Him the strength and wisdom to carry out His mission.

Before officially launching His ministry, Jesus went alone into the wilderness (Luke 4:1–14). Before choosing the twelve apostles, He went alone to the mountain and prayed the whole night (Luke 6:12–16). Before going to the cross, He went with a few of His disciples but prayed alone in the garden of Gethsemane (Matthew 22:36–46).

This is what Jesus did throughout His time on the earth. He always drew near to God by Himself and received power.

CONCLUSION

Whereas the previous chapters have focused on the power of God to do what our human minds may rule to be impossible, I now want to focus on what we must do, as believers, to activate and release God's power.

This is a call to action. If you want to take your walk with the Lord to another level, if you want to receive miracles that will open people's eyes in wonder, if you want to experience every aspect of God's power, then make up your mind. Go into your room, shut the door, and seek the Lord who can raise back to life those who are dead. The crowd is not yours. If you stay among them, they will kill your faith and instill confusion instead of confidence.

Paul knew this secret:

> But when it pleased God, who separated me from my mother's womb and called me through His grace, to reveal His Son in me, that I might preach Him among the Gentiles, I did not immediately confer with flesh and blood, nor did I go up to Jerusalem to those who were apostles before me; but I went to Arabia, and returned again to Damascus. (Galatians 1:15–17, NKJV)

For three years, he stayed in Arabia, praying alone, away from anyone who could influence his calling. He came out from a wilderness a filled vessel, ready to turn the world upside-down with the message of the gospel (Acts 17:6).

The secret is to go into your upper room, shut the door behind you, and not come out until He has filled you. We have His promise that we will find Him if we seek Him with all our hearts (Jeremiah 29:13).

Someone once said, "One-third of people will hate you for what you do, one-third won't care about what you do, and one-third will love you for what you do." Don't care about the two-thirds who will never understand you. Don't share with them your dream and ambition. Instead walk with the one-third who will support you.

God is merciful. He knows that we are social beings and will always give us people to walk with, even if they are few in number. They will go with you behind doors and help you raise your hands in prayer as you fight to possess what is yours by God's decree.

ABOUT THE AUTHOR

CHANTAL KABERUKA IS the founder and president of Life Equip and Empower (LEE), a not-for-profit organization incorporated in Canada whose mission is equipping and empowering women through Women Equip and Empower and youth through Youth Equip and Empower. LEE prepares and hosts Women Inspired, a bi-annual conference that seeks to empower professional women. LEE also organizes Girls' Roundtable events, which are debate and discussion events for college girls. She has been in the ministry for more than twenty-five years, alongside her husband. She also keeps a weekly Christian blog, mylifetothefullest.org, in which she shares everyday life experiences to encourage believers to live their lives to the fullest. She has more than twenty years of experience in academia and government institutions. She has initiated and implemented several projects for youth and women empowerment as part of her charitable endeavors. Chantal is a public speaker, with a passion for mentoring the youth. Her message is centered on the three action verbs: grow, connect, and lead. She resides in Ottawa with her family.